Approach it, Map it, Manage it.

The Graduated Response, Provision Mapping and Management

Book 2 – The SENDCO Solutions Support Series

APRIL 16, 2018

www.sendcosolutions.co.uk

A couple of notes:

SENDCO, SENCO, INCO, ALNCO, Vulnerable Groups Co-ordinator, LD Co-Ordinator, Inclusion Manager, SEN Coordinator (legal), etc. => **SENDCO/SENCO** (sorry if you use a different title.)

Student, Pupil, Child, Young Person, CYP, etc. => **Pupil**

TA, Teaching Assistant, LSA, Learning Support Assistant, LA, Learning Assistant, SNA, Special Needs Assistant, LM, Learning Mentor, Mentor, Support Assistant, etc. => **TA**

SLT, Senior Leadership Team, SMT, Senior Management Team, Higher Leadership, etc. => **SLT**

Headteacher, HT, Principal, Executive Principal, etc. => **Headteacher**

School, college, nursery, establishment, academy, etc. => **School**

Contents

Introduction

This book is split into three sections to represent the title: Approach  it, Map it, Manage It. The first part of the book explains the use of the Graduated Response (Approach). It will take you through the first 2 stages and can be applied to any pupils. Part two introduces Provision Mapping and the ideas behind this very useful recording tool and relates to stage 3 of the graduated response, doing. The final section moves us from creating the map to managing the map – the strategic management of our interventions and the final stage of the graduated response, reviewing.

(If you need additional information about Identification of Needs or making EHCP bids, please refer to other books in the series.)

Whilst the book is aimed at SENDCOs the duties of the Graduated Response are devolved to Class and Subject Teachers supported by TAs. Hopefully, this will provide you with enough background information to understand the role you play in each element.

I have been very careful to avoid suggesting you use any specific approach especially with regards to how you maintain your records. I certainly had my preferences (and I worked my way through many versions before settling on my final choices). Where screen shots have been used to illustrate points, they are taken from Learning Plans and Provision Maps (a product available

from   Edukey   Education   Ltd:
https://www.provisionmap.co.uk/)

Versions of any blank forms can be found at the back of this book and on the website. I find nothing more frustrating than seeing a good grid I fancy using then having to reproduce it myself. I've left them in Word format on the website, so you can adapt as you see fit, but pdf versions are also there if you just want something, 'off the shelf.'

As in my first book, The SENDCO, I will only give you background information if it is needed to understand each idea further.

I have a different style of writing to most SEN authors, preferring to illustrate the theory with examples from my experience in the role rather than get bogged down with technicalities. Hopefully, you will read this and recognise the pupils, staff or parents I describe!

I'm also a realist. I know you and your teaching staff are not perfect, your children do not perfectly fit examples and parents are rarely straightforward. I know what the SEN Code of Practice says you should do and it is our ultimate aim, but it isn't going to happen overnight – we need a culture change first, so let's be sensible and suggest what could work in the interim to put us on the right path.

The Children's and Family Act 2014 enthused me. I thought it took some exciting steps forward in developing SEN provision, especially inclusion. By the time the final version of the SEN Code of Practice (guidelines to ensure compliance with the Children's and Family Act) came out in January 2015 I'd given up the will and spent most nights in tears. Why? Because whilst I could see the advantage of changes I didn't have a supportive SLT and I had a teaching team too ingrained in their ways.

I was ready to change but I didn't have the skills set or support to kickstart anyone else. I knew what I wanted to do, but I had no power to make it happen. If this is you, then this book will resound with you.

Now, I market myself as an Educational Consultant and you may wonder how I can do that considering what I've just said...there are two keys things; I've walked the walk (via the prickly hedgerow) and the schools I work with WANT to make changes...now, that is something I can work with.

I read widely, but some books made me want to cry. It took me two years to pluck up the courage to open Natalie Packer's, The Perfect SENCO. Every book I read made the assumption that every teacher welcomes SEN pupils with open arms and they are delighted with the changes in the new SEN Code of Practice and up for the challenge of becoming the SEN specialist within their own room. I'm under no such illusion/delusion.

(PS: Natalie's book was great once I got past the title.)

Approach it
Plans, Notes, Communication

Schools are still required to keep clear records of a child's SEN, the provision put in place for them and the difference that support will make.

The SEN Code of Practice removed the need for a plan (IEP, Learning Plan Individual Education Plan, or whatever title you had adopted over the years), however it still requires a formal 'note' to be made. This note must be in an easily communicable format. In other words, if someone asks for the notes you need to be able to produce them in a format they can 'read'.

There are many ways to record the information. Some schools use their MIS to add a note, some have a proforma, handwritten document, others use a software program. I should admit to being in the latter category. My program allowed me to input the information I needed, share instantly with relevant staff, professionals and with the parents electronically, and was easily accessible by all involved.

Whether you choose to use a plan, one-page profile, passport or note on a provision or other system is up to you and your school. What is clear you need to have somewhere to store your information. With the launch of GDP in May 2018 there are additional implications. But what are you expected to record?

The SEN Code of Practice tells us that you must make a record of the conversation with parents about putting a pupil onto the SEN Register and about any provisions or targets that are agreed. In essence, although the need for a 'formal plan' is no longer a requirement you are still being asked to record the main ingredients of the plan.

Where shall we start?

The SENDCO should have created and checked the SEN register and made sure everyone knows who they are working with and why. A class teacher may be asked to double check this list in relation to their class. Once you've got your SEN list does this tally with what you thought you had?

Here is where we all need our SENDCO hats on. Who should be on that filtered SEN list? There is no reason why a class or subject teacher shouldn't challenge the list, in fact most SENDCOs would love this to happen

The SEN Code of Practice (2015)[1] bought about many changes but one of the key ones was around levels of SEN. Previously, we had been used to S, SA and SAP (Statements, School Action and School Action Plus). With the new code we had two new replacement levels; E (or EHCP) for Education, Health and Care Plans – effectively the new Statements, and K (I'll explain in a minute) for SEN Support, or everyone else identified as SEN. I suppose it's better than when I started out in SEN, there were five levels then with numbers.

It's interesting, I regularly get asked what certain codes mean within a school's own paperwork and very occasionally someone will ask where they come from. During a transition period the MIS systems needed a new code for pupils in receipt of SEN Support, but they couldn't use the codes already in there. The result was 'K'. I'm yet to find a suitable explanation as to why, but if you've ever looked at the codes in there, it was one of the few letters that would stand out as being new and hadn't been used previously.

This is probably a good point to explain what an MIS is, in case I confuse you! MIS – Management Information System. The market leader seems to be SIMS, but there are others out there such as CMIS, Bromcom, Integris, and Arbor. It's the electronic system that stores all your pupil data; things like addresses, contact information, their history and very often their

---

[1] https://www.gov.uk/government/publications/send-code-of-practice-0-to-25

attendance/registration marks. It's also the system used for running the reports needed for census. Even if you don't personally have access to the MIS (and use a paper attendance register in the classroom) it is likely you are asked at least once a year by the school business manager, bursar, data manager or Headteacher, to cross check information held within there.

The next few paragraphs explain the sen codes drawn from common mis and their meanings, feel free to skip if you already know this information.

S

STATEMENTED (SSEN). This code should not be in current use on your system after 31st March 2018 since all statements <u>should</u> have been converted to EHCPs! However, you may see it on old paperwork.

P

SCHOOL ACTION PLUS (you might also see this written as SAP or SA+) – this really shouldn't have been used after September 2014, but some schools took a little longer than others in updating their information. Of course, if you are looking at a child's history you will see it there. It was the code often used to signal those children who didn't have a statement but who needed significantly more support than other children in the school.   Some local authorities, including my own, advised it could only be used with children who received external or local authority support. For many pupils without a Statement of SEN, the P code was the only way to access not just the support but also additional funding.

a

SCHOOL ACTION (sometimes written as SA)– again this code should have disappeared by now and only be visible on older records. It was the code adopted for pupils who received SEN support but perhaps not so much as some of their peers. In quite a few schools it was the catch-all code – meaning those pupils who had a ''label' but needed nothing additional to or different from in terms of their provision were placed in

this group. This is, of course, not the definition of an SEN pupil in this SEN Code of Practice or the last one.

Ɛ

EDUCATION, HEALTH AND CARE PLAN (and often abbreviated to EHC or EHCP). This code replaced S and as all statements have been converted should be in your system. (I do say all statements have been converted as I am writing in the first week of April 2018, and the deadline for conversion was 31st March...!) It signifies the pupils in your school with the highest levels of need who have a legal document identifying those needs and stating exactly what must be done to meet them. Can I emphasise that it is a LEGAL status supported by a LEGAL document?

If you needed a rough estimate, approximately 1.3% of primary pupils and 1.7% of secondary pupils in a mainstream school will have this code. If you have an enhanced resource unit attached to your school, or a good reputation in the local area then you may find your number is much higher.   Whilst the percentages do vary year on year, as measured by census, they have stayed roughly similar for the last few years.

K

K is the letter now used instead of A and P. (Please do not, as I have heard one school do, refer to your "*Special K*" pupils!) With reference to the SEN Code of Practice it means **SEN SUPPORT**. It might be worth spending 10 minutes purging your MIS and making sure the current codes for pupils reflect this.

When the A and P codes were removed and amalgamated into the single K code the total percentage should have gone down as the lowest need pupils became supported through quality first teaching.   This has generally held true with 12.2% of primary and 14.4% of secondary pupils in a mainstream school under this code down from approximately 18 & 20%.   However, in areas of high deprivation and those with weak primary school provision the numbers can rapidly increase. It is always worth asking your local authority for their average SEN percentages and questioning yourself as to whether you are over, or under-identifying needs in your school.

$\mathcal{N}$

This code has caused many a headache over the years.

When it was first introduced it was used for any pupil who didn't have an SEN designation (in other words, **NO SEN**.) This was because the original MIS programs couldn't handle an empty field.

Over time, the use has changed and the majority of schools now use it to designate a child who was SEN previously but is now not designated as such (**NO LONGER SEN**).

I prefer this use, it signals which pupils may be at risk and need additional support in the future.

You will have to ask your school business manager (or whoever controls your MIS) how they use the code in your school.

$\mathcal{M}$

This isn't a standard code, but so many schools use it, I feel it needs mentioning here.

Most schools use it to mean **MONITORING**. A pupil who isn't in receipt of SEN support, or perhaps doesn't really hit the criteria, but staff are concerned about. It is used in many schools for those who perhaps used to be A but were 'lost' from the system in the SEN Code of Practice changes.

Beware though, some schools use it to mean **MEDICAL** need. Again, check with your MIS manager.

O

Other Letters. Well, really there shouldn't be any, but you can bet the odd one or two pop up. They will have come from some well-intentioned individual/school trying to 'code' things more effectively.

I've seen *EAL* (do I need to remind you EAL is not on its own an SEN?), *T* (for **TARGETED** – I'm not sure what I'm targeting, although it could be a school-determined level within K?) and *U* (**UNKNOWN**, no, I mean unknown, I have no idea what information the school was trying to convey with the 23/378 pupils it had coded U under the SEN level, although I suspect it was using it to signify **UNDERACHIEVING**, which again is not an SEN code.)

It is important that you know how your school is operating since the codes are used during census and if you were not aware census drive a good degree of your school funding for the following academic years.

So, how do you determine which of your pupils should be on the register? Let us remind ourselves what the SEN Code of Practice tells us...

Definition of SEN from the Code of Practice...

A child or young person has SEN if they have a learning difficulty or disability which calls for special educational provision to be made for him or her.

A child of compulsory school age or a young person has a learning difficulty or disability if he or she:

• has a significantly greater difficulty in learning than the majority of others of the same age, or

• has a disability which prevents or hinders him or her from making use of facilities of a kind generally provided for others of the same age in mainstream schools or mainstream post-16 institutions

For children aged two or more, special educational provision is educational or training provision that is additional to or different from that made generally for other children or young people of the same age by mainstream schools, maintained nursery schools, mainstream post-16 institutions or by relevant early years providers. For a child under two years of age, special educational provision means educational provision of any kind.

A child under compulsory school age has special educational needs if he or she is likely to fall within the definition above when they reach compulsory school age or would do so if special educational provision was not made for them (Section 20 Children and Families Act 2014).

Post-16 institutions often use the term learning difficulties and disabilities (LDD). The term SEN is used in the Code across the 0-25 age range but includes LDD.

This means, you should be 'coding' as SEN any pupil for whom you are putting in place interventions which are different from, or additional to, those which most of the school access.

So – a homework club, a lunchtime chess group, a reading volunteer open to all pupils is not an SEN provision, although SEN pupils may well still access it. However, if your pupil is accessing the provision more frequently than others, needs the materials adapting, or has to do the intervention differently (perhaps 1:1 instead of a small group) then this is different from/additional to.

Of course, SEN'ness (is that a word?) is not defined by the interventions we put in place – but does give us a good measure to work with.

Contentiously, the other criteria commonly applied is any 'label' a child has been given. If a paediatrician has gone to the trouble of diagnosing a child as on the Autistic Spectrum or an Educational Psychologist tells you about a processing difficulty, then they are already indicating to you that the child has a special need which needs to be met in your school. Ironically, it is often the 'label' which drives parents to request their child is on our SEN register, regardless of whether their label means they need any form of Special Educational Provision to be made. Whilst this may be the right decision for some pupils, it is not appropriate for all. There was a lot of research reported on towards the end of 2017 about how labels are not always helpful. They come with pre-conceptions (usually of behaviour and academic expectations) which can be difficult to shift. Some families believe that the label will bring extra support, exams concessions or even money whereas others are after the comfort blanket of being able to describe why their child 'is the way they are' with a single word or short phrase.

Personally, I've always found the 'label' helpful for me as the SENDCO in reminding me and teaching staff of general strategies required to meet the needs of that pupil. However, as every pupil is different, the strategies offered by a label are not individualised enough, but a starting point. Framed in a positive manner, it can be useful in discussion with parents and pupils about their strengths as well as why they experience difficulties in some areas. Even the negatives can be the 'coat hanger' upon which to hang the problems experienced on a daily basis.

Frustratingly though, I have seen the other side of labels being applied and the child living their life to the label. One lovely, young lady was labelled at the age of 5 as having dyslexia (her much older brother had been recently diagnosed and the family feeling guilty at not having noticed sooner were understandably looking for all the little signs. Based on this, school had arranged an assessment for her, concluding she was a little behind her peers.) Now, I don't think that at 5 a child has had enough exposure and experience with language and literacy to make that diagnosis or apply that label but that's my opinion. Anyway, move forward a few years. Her lovely primary school had given her 1:1 support in all lessons where she needed to read or write. She was highly dependent on that support. When assessed at age 9 she was significantly behind her peers. Effectively, four years of being told, "you won't be able to do that," and, "I'll do that bit for you," meant she couldn't do it. Oddly enough, the subjects where she received no support at primary (Art and PE) she was highly confident, even when trying reading and writing tasks. It took 5 years of unpicking at secondary to convince her that she was able to do it for herself, unfortunately she was, by this point, several years behind her peers, not with the incapacity to learn but just the missing time from opportunities, so it only took the slightest thing to knock her confidence and make her revert back to her 'learned helplessness'.

Definition of 'D' from the Code of Practice...

Many children and young people who have SEN may have a disability under the Equality Act 2010 – that is '...a physical or mental impairment which has a long-term and substantial adverse effect on their ability to carry out normal day-to-day activities'. This definition provides a relatively low threshold and includes more children than many realise: 'long-term' is defined as 'a year or more' and 'substantial' is defined as 'more than minor or trivial'. This definition includes sensory impairments such as those affecting sight or hearing, and long-term health conditions such as asthma, diabetes, epilepsy, and cancer. Children and young people with such conditions do not necessarily have SEN, but there is a significant overlap between disabled children and young people and those with SEN. Where a disabled child or young person requires special educational provision, they will also be covered by the SEN definition.

If a pupil breaks their hand and has it in a cast for 2 weeks, followed by a few weeks with a bandage, they are not disabled using this definition! It is neither long-term nor substantial.

On the other (unbroken) hand, a pupil who sustains a head injury may have long term difficulties and although not visible they can lead to substantial problems.

More obviously, a pupil with a hearing impairment will need their classroom needs and the environment addressing.

It is easy to forget our pupils with 'daily' medical needs which are also covered by the legislation (and more recently have been bought to our attention with reports about how schools are failing to meet the medical needs of their pupils.)

The SENDCO (sorry, you are responsible for medical needs, even if you are not a first aider) needs to communicate this information to other members of the school community. I recall a young man who didn't want anyone to know about his diabetes. He managed it very well and needed no support from us with regards to checking his glucose levels. Whilst we agreed he didn't meet our criteria for SEN, we did agree that his teaching staff and the first aiders needed to know so that as a school we could discharge our duty of care. He decided to write a letter that we then shared with the appropriate staff.

There is little dispute who belongs on your register as an 'E', since their provision is set out in law. We come to information about applying for EHCPs later in the series of books although they are briefly touched upon in here. I suspect your 'D' pupils are obvious too (place them at E, K or Medical as appropriate). The vagueness is with who you place at 'K'.

It has always fascinated me that a pupil placed on the SEN register in one school, might not actually be on the SEN register in another school. This has a lot to do with the Quality First Teaching which every pupil is entitled to, but the 'quality' of which can vary considerably. However, it can also be down to the way lower level, but high incidence, needs are met within the school. If we take, for example, the two schools below we can see how their different approach to the same cohort of pupils can result in 3 times as many pupils being on one register compared to the other.

Of course, no school cohort is ever this simple...if only.

Meet School A: This school has 100 pupils in Y7. 15 of them have a reading age below 8yrs on entry to the school. The school decides to create a new teaching group for those pupils across the whole of their curriculum and deliver all their lessons using an upper KS2 approach and limited class teachers with the support of a TA. 5 of the individuals in the class have needs other than their low reading age (which are met through other interventions) and are placed on the SEN register. The remainder of the pupils are placed on monitor to see if there is any reason for the deficit in their reading ages. As they are all receiving the same intervention and quality first teaching there is no need to place them on the SEN register at this stage.

The advantage is this approach is that there is a small number of staff involved who will know the pupils well. A quality first teaching approach being used to meet the majority of their needs. This method allows for monitoring (and maturing) and additional information to be gathered. There is efficient use of a single TA and a supportive, familiar environment.

Unfortunately, 15 is still a large group for pupils. There is likely to be less individualisation or differentiation as the needs are all deemed similar. Movement from the group can be difficult both to timetable and to achieve and banding "like with like" often means good role models are lost.

In terms of the SEN register 5/15 pupils are placed on there at stage K (or above)

Meet School B: This school also has 100 pupils in Y7 with 15 of them having a reading age below 8yrs on entry to the school. The school doesn't have the capacity to create a new group so the pupils are taught the same way as the rest of the pupils in the school, in mixed ability classes. Where possible there is a TA deployed to their classes who prioritises support for the 5 pupils with other needs but from whom any pupils can request help as required. Pupils are withdrawn for additional literacy sessions in groups of 4 and some have 1:1 reading in the morning. All 15 pupils receive something that is delivered small group or 1:1. As a result, all 15 pupils are placed on the SEN register.

This approach means that pupils are fully included in the school. The interventions are tailored for the individuals rather than the group. Movement between teaching groups can be achieved more easily and cater towards strengths (art/maths) as well as difficulties.

Unfortunately, there are larger group sizes, variability in staff (names and their styles), withdrawal can cause issues, and they may not receive enough support if they are not in a supported class. There is less 'time' spent on meeting their needs, although the time that is spent is 'quality over quantity'. Peers can pick up on 'differences' and are not always nice about it.

15/15 pupils are on the SEN register.

This only goes to show the disparity caused by the definition of SEN as being in receipt of different from/additional to provision.

Anyone who has taught in more than one school will know that they can be vastly different. I recall admitting a pupil to our inner-city secondary school following a house move from a leafy, village school. In his village school his reading age, 6 months behind his chronological age, had him receiving 1:1 intervention for 15 minutes every morning, a comprehension club after school once a week and a TA in his English and humanities lessons. He had disengaged from his lessons and was refusing to attend school prior to the house move.

In the inner-city secondary, he was placed in top sets and with the family we agreed to monitor him for the first 6 weeks to see how he did without any support. It was a tricky decision, we had lots of notes from the village school telling us about all the support this pupil apparently needed. Truth be told, we just didn't have the resources to put that level of support in place for him, and as a Y8 working at old National Curriculum levels 6-7 across the board we really didn't feel he needed it.

Six weeks in, we reviewed progress. He had 100% attendance, was enjoying school, was 4 months behind with his reading age (if you looked at standard score he was securely in the normal range and above 90) and he was delighted to discover that he was one of the brightest in the year group rather than being made to feel he was one of the weakest.

Our conclusion, he did not need to be on our SEN register!

This is a positive story, but one that goes to illustrate that it is the environment and establishment that will determine a pupil's SEN'ness as much as any label will.

At the opposite end of the scale, we once admitted a pupil who had no needs from a local secondary school (the school was due to close at the end of the academic year and pupils were slowly transferring to others in the area). The school admitted he was slightly 'quirky' but no different to other pupils in his class, working at the highest levels in there, and not in receipt of any support beyond the odd reminder to stop daydreaming. He was not, in their opinion, an SEN pupil.

Within 3 weeks of starting with us, everything had broken down. He was refusing to attend, couldn't cope in the classroom, was not able to access any of the work despite being in our lower ability groupings (with 15 pupils and about 50% of the lessons TA supported). Why?

It turns out that his previous school hadn't been entirely forthcoming with information about his classes. He probably wasn't as 'SEN' as others in there but there were only 9 pupils in his class, 2 of whom had part-time timetables (don't go there!) They were supported by the same TA for every lesson and often there was an additional TA deployed, meaning a 3:1 ratio of pupil:adult in many of his lessons. The other school didn't consider this unusual. As they were closing down at the end of the year and many of their pupils were moving on, classes were shrinking in size and staff redeployed as they were contracted until the Summer.

Eventually, this young man became a complete school refuser, despite our best efforts, and we requested a Section 323 (old Statement). He didn't get one, but we did get a Notice In Lieu, which advised various suggestions. I'd love to say there was a happy ending, but by Y11 he was a recluse in his bedroom which I'm sad to say was not exactly encouraged, but certainly not challenged, by his family. Although, as a school, we advised against it, they had decided by Y9 that he would be better 'home educated'.

I'd like at this point to clarify the difference between the Graduated Approach and the Graduated Response. The two terms are used interchangeably and are talking about the same thing – the process through which we move in establishing a pupil's needs and the actions we take.

The Approach results in us following a series of steps. The Response results in us determining the SEN'ness and the details within the steps. In essence, like most authors I'll probably end up using both terms.

Back to my first foray into SEN the Graduated Response (although I don't recall it being called this) was the result of moving through the levels of SEN'ness, there were 5 levels this was quite straightforward:

1- We think there is a problem, let's keep an eye on it

2- We are going to try this classroom intervention

3- We need to put something a bit more individualised in place

4- We need the advice/support of an external professional

5- OK – give us a statement, we are struggling to meet the needs of this child and need lots of support and advice

In those days it was unusual to come back down the scale, once you were on there you tended to work your way up the numbers until you were eventually allocated the one at which you made progress and then you stayed there, regardless of whether you still needed to be at that level 5 years later.

With the 2004 SEN Code of Practice and the three levels there was introduced this idea that you could move up AND down the levels as needed. It was still unusual to get a Statement and then drop back down to School Action Plus – but not completely unheard of. (I had one pupil who definitely needed a Statement whilst at primary school, but as he matured and as he met staff more equipped to deal with his needs, he didn't need it by the time he reached Y9. In fact, I suspect if he hadn't obtained a Statement whilst at primary school I probably wouldn't have even had him on my SEN radar by Y9!)

In its simplest terms the old codes gave us:

A – This pupil needs some help to meet their needs

P – This pupil needs a lot of help to meet their needs (and in some local authorities this code could only be used if they also accessed support from professionals outside the school. Pupils generally had to be at P level to access any additional funding.)

S – This pupil needs a full assessment of their needs and the ongoing support of professionals to meet their needs.

Movement on and off the register and between A and P was common.

The newest SEN Code of Practice only gives us two levels to play with. E and K. Believe me, if you have managed to get as far as the E level you are probably not going to come down to a K with any haste! There will have been a lot of battles fought, hours wasted and tears shed in getting the EHCP. Keep it and let the local authority do their job in maintaining it (it's their job to ensure everything in there is done, not yours, you 'coordinate' that element, more on that later.)

With only level K to look at, you are working with a number of pupils (if you were in role before 2014 then it is effectively all of your A and P pupils probably minus a few of the As that you now just keep an eye on.) You may well move pupils on and off K, although I suspect this is something that you probably undertake less frequently than the movements between A and P were historically. It should be reviewed regularly, let's set a target of three times a year when we review the plans and provisions, but let's also be realistic and state we will do it a minimum of once a year!

I have the pleasure of working with many schools and I often see an 'unofficial scaling' within the K level.   Some schools have gone to a 'tiered' approach with 2, 3 or even 6 levels within their 'K'. I'm not advocating this at all, but it can be helpful to have in your own head the level of 'K'ness' a pupil is at. A pupil who is likely to eventually need an EHCP or Element 3 funding will require lots of planning, additional support and record keeping in order to evidence your application. A pupil with low level needs may only need 1-2 terms of interventions in Y1 and has completely vanished from your register by Y4.

The Graduated Approach/Response

Many of us know the Graduated Approach as the 'Assess, Plan, Do, Review' Cycle.

Now, you may be wondering why I haven't shown this as the traditional 'cycle'. That's because after the review you need to do something else – you need to **make a decision** and based on that decision you will determine your re-entry point or exit from the cycle itself.

Examples: Let's use our Y7s with low reading ages from earlier.

They all enter a reading intervention for a 6-week period, at the end of which we gather further data to review.

1: When reviewing, a pupil has met all targets and objectives, is now working at (or beyond) age related expectations across all subjects. They are no longer in receipt of additional to/different from support and therefore they can be removed from the SEN Register. Therefore, they exit the cycle completely.

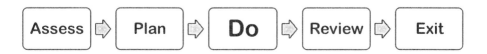

2: Upon review we discover that the last cycle of intervention didn't go ahead as the pupil was absent for 6 weeks on a family holiday (!) We have no further data to assess, the plan (and their needs) are still the same, so they re-enter the cycle at the Do stage.

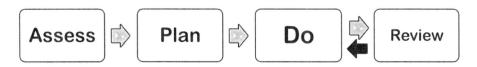

3: This pupil has just had an optician's appointment two weeks into the intervention process and been given a quite strong prescription for lenses and a recommendation of using a coloured overlay. They hadn't made progress with the interventions saying they couldn't do it. (Or more likely couldn't see it!) A decision is made to re-write the plan considering the new information. We don't need to do any more assessment. Re-enter at the Plan stage and advise all teachers of the additional information.

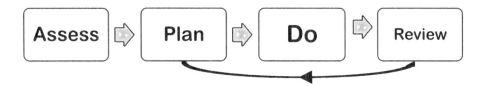

4: Our final pupil has completed the cycle, but made limited progress despite the quality interventions put in place. We need to look again at their needs, possibly do more observations and try to pin down what needs to take place in order for them to progress. This pupil re-enters at the Assess stage.

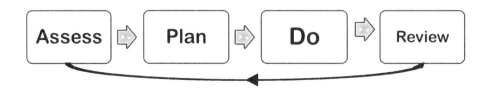

So, the whole system is dynamic. We might aim to review on a particular date, but in reality, we need to be on top of our information and adapt our schedule and approach.

Here is a silly, but illustrative example...

You put in place an intervention that runs every morning for 20 minutes with a trained TA. It is planned to take place throughout the whole year. You have set the formal review (i.e. collection of end data and reporting on progress) to take place at the end of the year.

Now ask yourself a question. Would you teach 180 lessons before marking or looking at the children's books?

Of course, the answer is, 'No.' You probably wouldn't go more than 5 lessons without checking. But we know you don't have time to check in on every intervention, every day. However, the TA delivering that intervention could provide some information every 5-10 sessions. You would start to get some feedback on whether the intervention is working and if it isn't you have the chance to address why.

This demonstrates the importance of everyone being aware of their role in the Graduated Approach.

More information about each stage of the graduated approach can be found in the next few chapters.

Assess

This is not 'assessment' in the sense of a test or exam, although it may include data from these.

When assessing a pupil with Special Educational Needs we are using our knowledge and data about the child to 'assess' or determine where their needs lie. This can include looking at notes from professionals, other teachers, diagnostic assessments, records over time and observations in the classroom.

The SEN Code of Practice says that the assessment process is three-fold; it has a clear analysis of the child's needs, information from the school's assessment and experience of the pupil, and parent/pupil views.

6.45 In identifying a child as needing SEN support the class or subject teacher, working with the SENCO, should carry out a clear analysis of the pupil's needs. This should draw on the teacher's assessment and experience of the pupil, their previous progress and attainment, as well as information from the school's core approach to pupil progress, attainment, and behaviour. It should also draw on other subject teachers' assessments where relevant, the individual's development in comparison to their peers and national data, the views and experience of parents, the pupil's own views and, if relevant, advice from external support services. Schools should take seriously any concerns raised by a parent. These should be recorded and compared to the setting's own assessment and information on how the pupil is developing.

6.46 This assessment should be reviewed regularly. This will help ensure that support and intervention are matched to need, barriers to learning are identified and overcome, and that a clear picture of the interventions put in place and their effect is developed. For some types of SEN, the way in which a pupil responds to an intervention can be the most reliable method of developing a more accurate picture of need.

6.47 In some cases, outside professionals from health or social services may already be involved with the child. These professionals should liaise with the school to help inform the assessments. Where professionals are not already working with school staff the SENCO should contact them if the parents agree.

The SEN Code of Practice requires you to make a note of these assessments and any discussions. I always preferred a formal template for this, but you could add a note within the MIS. I make sure my section is headed ASSESS and I will record everything I've used in making any decisions (or evidence presented in discussions.) As I mentioned in an earlier chapter I still use and refer to this as a 'plan', because that is what I'm doing – I'm creating a 'plan of action' with my information on it.

Assess isn't just about numerical data though…it's about information. And before you can record the information you need to gather it. This information will come from a variety of sources and tempting though it is to rely on 'professional' information, the input of parents and pupils is just as useful/valuable.

Parents & Wider Family	The Pupil	SENDCO	TAs
Class/ Subject Teachers	Dinner staff	Social Worker	Family Support Worker
Speech & Language Therapist	CAMHS	Paediatrician/GP	Specialist Nurses
Educational Psychologist	Occupational Therapist	Play/Art Therapist	Counsellor
Specialist Teachers	Physiotherapy	Others…	

You need to have a mechanism in place to gather this information. Some of it will be in formal written reports (don't forget to store the original in the pupil's file), some of it will be gathered through discussions with the individuals involved.

Don't forget that GDPR means we need to be clear with people what purpose their information will serve!

The assess stage is the first formalisation of an SEN process so you will be asking for parental permission to include their child. This is best done face to face so you could gather their views at a meeting to add them to the plan. Subsequent reviews can check the information and amend where appropriate.

Despite using technology for many years to support my role, I'm afraid I still resort to a good old piece of paper and the odd checklist to help me at times. This is one of those times, since I need to be sure I'm gathering all the information I might need to truly reflect the needs of the child I'm working with.

So what kind of information might we be looking for? We are looking to paint a picture of the child. One that tells us about their strengths and difficulties.

Teacher assessments	Teacher experiences	Pupil progress & attainment data	Behaviour information
A comparison to peers	Views of parents	Experiences of parents	Views of the pupil
Standardised tests	Criterion-referenced assessments	Checklists	Profile information
Advice from external services	Observations	Questionnaires (pupil, parents, professionals)	Screening assessments

This is not an exhaustive list and there are likely many other pieces of information you will use. It is quite clear that some of this information may be at our finger-tips but that some of it comes from alternative sources.

There are two quick deviations I want to take at this point...one is a foray into specialist assessments and the other is a dive into initial concerns.

I have a whole book dedicated to specialist assessments, so the only thing I want to say here, is that whilst we may want to minimise the amount of additional testing we put a pupil through we need to be secure in the judgements we are making and establishing baselines from which we can make judgements about outcomes and progress. If you choose your assessments wisely you will find that they can serve a multitude of purposes. A really decent spelling test can be used across your whole cohort to give you an indicator of the whole group and the individual, it sets a baseline for any intervention and can be reported on in both the plan and the intervention. A parallel or repeat test after a period of time will give us the information needed to make our progress judgements.

Initial concerns are those expressed before a child becomes a part of the SEN Register. Whilst most teachers will come running as soon as they spot a problem, they often haven't tried any alternative methods to meet needs first. Having a good initial concerns form can be really helpful in making sure that teachers have the confidence to try things in their classroom first and also gives you more evidence of the staged approach to SEN. Remember that the SEN Code of Practice puts meeting the needs of SEN pupils firmly in the hands of the class and subject teachers.

I've included a paper version of the initial checklist I used to use across most of my settings.

Initial Concerns record

I am concerned about a pupil in my class.

Name: _____

I teach this pupil for: _____ **over** _____ **hours/week.**

I have observed the following difficulties:

The pupil demonstrates the following strengths:

They need further assistance with:

I have tried the following to assist them, some worked better than others:

Strategy	*Did it work?*

Member of staff completing this form: _____

Date completed: _____

Extracting information from professional reports

Professionals are brilliant at providing very wordy reports and it will be up to you as the SENDCO to extract from those reports the information that is needed, not only to support your planning for the pupil (and inform your teaching staff) but often to support parents in understanding what professionals are saying about their child. I have lost count of how many reports I've had to translate into parent-speak because the professionals don't have time to explain things. One family used to record conversations, with the paediatrician consent, and bring them to me for an explanation. Another used to ask me to make their appointments at a time I could go with them in order to support. (And no, it isn't a normal and expected part of the role, but it enabled me to gain a greater insight into the pupils needs, so why would I refuse?)

Some reports are not the easiest documents to read or understand, although I promise you do get better with experience (and a decent dictionary). I am convinced a background in science has helped me immensely over the years! Here are a couple of examples.

Hearing

A hearing assessment report may include reference to an audiogram. ('Audio' means 'sound' and 'gram' means 'picture' so we are looking at a sound picture, or graph.) A typical audiogram plots Decibels of hearing loss (how loud a sound has to be for us to hear it) against Pitch (whether it's a low note or a high note.) With normal hearing we can hear sounds from -10 to 20 dB on the scale and across a range of pitches from 125 to 8000 Hz. As soon as we begin to suffer hearing loss we need to increase the number of decibels in order to hear the same sound. Sometimes this only affects sounds at one end of the pitch, for others it may be across the range. Mild hearing loss is identified when the sounds need to be 20-40 dB to be heard, Moderate hearing loss for 40-70 dB, Severe hearing loss at 70-95 dB and Profound hearing loss at above 95dB. Each ear might be different.

To illustrate an example: I lost the hearing in my right ear at the age of 18 following a viral infection, it is across the range of pitch. I'm also getting a little older and suffering from typical old person hearing loss,

I blame noisy classrooms! My left ear I need sounds to be above 21 dB across the pitches for them to be audible, but in my right ear I need them to be above 65 dB. (I do have a slight variation across the pitches, but these numbers will do for the illustration.) So, I have a 'mild' hearing loss in my left ear meaning that I can usually hear what people say although may struggle to pick their exact words out in a noisy environment. In my right ear, I have a moderate hearing loss meaning speech lacks clarity; I can hear you but I can't always work out what you are saying and when you face away from me it is very difficult. I can best describe it as being under water with a soggy duvet on my head. In the classroom, then, I am better placed so that anyone who is speaking to me is towards my left side and facing me. I often complain about my husband's music as all I can hear is the base line and a droning sound, which is apparently someone singing!

Vision

A visual report is likely to include some strange medical terms such as nystagmus, aphakia, glioma, myopia and acuity. I'm a scientist so they don't bother me too much, but even so I like to sit with my glossary to hand and effectively rewrite the report in 'layman's English'. Here is a typical prose from a 'functional vision assessment'.

The most recent eye report, dated August 5, 2017, gives a visual acuity of 20/400 at both near and distance without correction. Correction and/or treatment are not applicable. According to this report his eye condition is stable. X has a visual diagnosis of aniridia plus (incomplete formation of the iris, retina and optic nerve resulting in an acuity of 20/200 or greater), a coloboma (a small hole) of the retina OD (right), anomalous optic nerve OS (left), microphthalmia (smaller than usual eyes) esotropia (inward turning of the eyes), exotropia (outward turning of the eyes), pendular nystagmus (involuntary side-to-side movement) and high myopia (nearsightedness). Corrective lenses were prescribed on a trial basis to possibly aid in the pupil's myopia. Additionally, X is consistently monitored for cataracts and glaucoma.

And that means, actually this is a half-decent report, they've made an attempt to describe some of the terms...beyond the physical abnormality of his eye structure, X has wobbly eyes so finds it difficult to focus on one thing or to move his focus from one to another (board to book), they will often swing in the wrong direction to where he is looking and the only thing in this list that can be corrected for with lenses is his myopia (can't see long distances).

My third son was born with a cataract on his eye and this is not corrected for, in fact you wouldn't know he had it, except I just told you. He wears sunglasses as he can be a little more sensitive in bright light, and he has started to notice his vision in one eye is fuzzier if asked to close his other eye, but if he tips his head he can compensate for it, he's 7. The report from his ophthalmologist was far more school/parent friendly than the one above, it simply said, 'wear sunglasses in bright light, avoid fluorescent lighting and aim for natural light, avoid glare, take care during activities where the vision of one side might be impaired (such as in sports when navigating people and objects), report any headaches.'

I can only assure you that with practice, pulling the information you need from reports becomes easier. If you ever get the chance to sit down with one of the sensory team who have produced the report ask them to annotate a photocopy to explain the terms they use and what they mean. You'll be able to use it next time. Alternatively, ask other SENDCOs in your area or reach out on Twitter or SENDCO Forum for support. Someone is always there who will be able to help and it is important we understand the information we are being given.

Other reports that sometimes need 'interpretation' include those from Educational Psychology (make sure you understand basic psychology terminology and standardised scores), Physiotherapy (human anatomy lessons may be in order) and Speech & Language therapy.

Presentation of information
Once I have all the information it needs to be used and presented in a way that is helpful. I like to sort my information into Strengths and Concerns as this can help us see a whole picture of the pupil.

The current trend is for one-page profiles or passports and you often need to choose suitable headings. I'm yet to be sold on this being the only information I need as a teacher to meet the needs of a pupil. I'm all for pupil voice and the passport is a great way for them to convey some information to me in language they understand, but I actually need more

than they give me. Suitable headings could be: I learn best when...What I find difficult is...I am good at...Things that help me are...

ASSESS
Areas of Strength
Molly is a strong auditory learner. She is good humoured and friendly with her peers. She has had 100% attendance for the last 7 years. She likes to listen for patterns in things: e.g. rhyming words. She makes good use of acronyms and mnemonics to support her learning. She has excellent relationships with her teaching assistant and buddies. She will chat readily with a small group of friends and adults she knows. She greatly enjoys Australian soap operas!
Areas of Concern
Molly experiences difficulty with information presented in a written or illustrative format. Across the range of subjects Molly is working 2-3 years below her age-related expectations. Molly is reluctant to wear her prescription glasses as she says they give her a fuzzy head. Molly has difficulty understanding instructions and the requirements of tasks. She is not too great at acquiring sequencing skills - for example when following a recipe or science experiment. She has a difficulty understanding how she affects and can relate to her immediate surroundings. Her personal organisation over the short medium and long term is weak. Her reading age is 3 years below her chronological age. Her writing is slow, even on a laptop and her motor co-ordination is not good.
Assessment Data
Most information from parents/pupil and previous school advice. Reading assessment (LAO) 1.4.18 – Std Score 75. (Used green screen overlay) Other formal assessment dates booked.

Or as a passport:

I learn best when...	What I find difficult is...
Information is spoken to me. You use mnemonics, acronyms and word patterns	Using visual information, reading and pictures Wearing my glasses Understanding instructions and remembering their order Writing – I'm slow
I am good at...	**Things that help me are...**
Australian soap operas – I'd like to do a topic on them Talking through ideas and answers Learning facts by repetition, especially if they have a pattern.	Wearing my glasses! Using green overlays or paper Giving me instructions one at a time.

My recent results...	
Reading test – 75	

This brings me onto the next key concept (after the SEN levels) in the SEN world...the Areas of Need.

Areas of Need

There are only four BROAD Areas of Need in the SEN Code of Practice, although they allow for sub-categorisation. It is recognised that many difficulties are co-morbid (they come along with other difficulties) so it is common to use the phrases Primary Need and Secondary Needs.

The Areas of Need are set in law and you are required to report your SEN primary and secondary needs in each area for census. Therefore, it is important to make sure you are putting information into the correct places.

These are the four areas of need in the SEN Code of Practice:

~ Cognition and Learning
~ Communication and Interaction
~ Social, Emotional and Mental Health (this replaced Behavioural, Emotional and Social Difficulties of the previous SEN Code of Practice)
~ Sensory and Physical Difficulties

One of my other books has many sections describing common difficulties and disabilities along with their suggested broad area of need and sub-category, this is supported with checklists, suggested diagnostic assessments and advice on meeting those needs. The broad areas are, however, briefly covered here to save you hunting for another book!

The areas are often coded C&L, C&I, SEMH and SPD. Immediately someone will point out that more common abbreviations such as ADHD, ASD, VI, SpLD are not here. That's because they are sub-categories of SEMH, C&I, SPD and C&L respectively. (I often think SENDCOs should be awarded a diploma for being able to speak in a foreign language!) If you are unsure, there is a glossary of abbreviations in Book 1b.

Whilst you will look across the full range of assess information available to you, I have tried to indicate what must be included for a rounded assessment within each area. That's not to say behaviour isn't important for pupils who have Cognition and Learning Needs, indeed it may well be their behaviour that initially flagged a concern, it is however their academic data that will determine the 'need' and relevant intervention.

Cognition and Learning (C&L)
The SEND Code of Practice says:

6.30 Support for learning difficulties may be required when children and young people learn at a slower pace than their peers, even with appropriate differentiation. Learning difficulties cover a wide range of needs, including moderate learning difficulties (MLD), severe learning difficulties (SLD), where children are likely to need support in all areas of the curriculum and associated difficulties with mobility and communication, through to profound and multiple learning difficulties (PMLD), where children are likely to have severe and complex learning difficulties as well as a physical disability or sensory impairment.

6.31 Specific learning difficulties (SpLD) affect one or more specific aspects of learning. This encompasses a range of conditions such as dyslexia, dyscalculia and dyspraxia.

SEND Code of Practice p97

Cognition is the process of acquiring knowledge and understanding through thoughts, experiences, and senses. In describing cognition, we are using words such as knowledge, attention, memory and working memory, judgment and evaluation, reasoning and computation, problem solving and decision making, comprehension and production of language.

It is through our cognition that we develop our learning and thus move our skills forward.

The most common C&L difficulties we see in mainstream schools are

~ MLD – Moderate Learning Difficulties (sometimes called Mild Learning Difficulties although there is no clear guidance on which is the correct term to use. Bob Bates in his book *A Quick Guide to Special Needs and Disabilities* p156 (ISBN: 978-1473979741): suggests Mild Learning Difficulties is where a child has an IQ in the 50-70 range (2 standard deviations below 'average') or a mental age of 10-12 years on leaving school...Moderate Learning Difficulties is where the IQ is in the 35-50 range

(3 standard deviations below average) or a mental age of 8-10 years on leaving school. Whilst this is useful, for me it leaves out the chunk of children with an IQ in the 70-85 range (one standard deviation below average) which is considered 'below average'.) IQ testing is controversial, at best, but does provide a useful characteristic and supply a valuable piece of snapshot data.

The DFE says: Pupils with moderate learning difficulties will have: attainments significantly below expected levels in most areas of the curriculum despite appropriate interventions, needs that are not met by normal differentiation and flexibilities of the curriculum, much greater difficulty than their peers in acquiring basic literacy and numeracy skills difficulty understanding concepts, working memory and concentration difficulties, a possibility of having speech and language delay and under developed social skills. This is in fitting with our definition of cognition.

~ SpLD – Specific Learning Difficulties cover many of our 'Dys-' needs, for example dyscalculia, dyslexia, dyspraxia. They are needs related to the cognitive difficulties, but are only manifesting or affecting a specific area of learning. ADD/ADHD (Attention Deficit Disorder and Attention Deficit Hyperactivity Disorder) are sometimes grouped here too, since it is the difficulties with attention, memory and decision making which characterise these conditions. In the old SEN Code of Practice ADD/ADHD was often lumped into the BESD (Behavioural, Emotional and Social Difficulties) section due to the way the needs of children with these difficulties manifest themselves. (However, note the wording in the SEMH section of the SEN Code of Practice since this is where the Code recommends they are included.)

When gathering information for the Assess part of the Graduated Approach you will be looking at academic achievement and standardised scores, possibly within specific areas but generally across the board. If this is the first time you are putting the pupil on the SEN register then you will likely need screening assessments and may have some specialist exports. You are likely to be generalising comparisons to their peers.

An example...Our pupil is in Y8 and has a global learning delay. Data gathered:

- ~ Reading age (and standard score), Spelling age (and standard score), Single word reading standard score. Individual results and average for his teaching group.
- ~ CTOPP (Comprehensive Test of Phonological Processing) subtest standard score results for phoneme isolation, memory for digits, elision.
- ~ CAT4 scores (MSAS (the mean), Quantitative, Spatial, Non-verbal, Verbal.
- ~ Educational Psychology report including BPVS scores.

Communication and Interaction (C&I)
The SEND Code of Practice says:

6.28 Children and young people with speech, language and communication needs (SLCN) have difficulty in communicating with others. This may be because they have difficulty saying what they want to, understanding what is being said to them or they do not understand or use social rules of communication. The profile for every child with SLCN is different and their needs may change over time. They may have difficulty with one, some or all of the different aspects of speech, language or social communication at different times of their lives.

6.29 Children and young people with ASD, including Asperger's Syndrome and Autism, are likely to have particular difficulties with social interaction. They may also experience difficulties with language, communication and imagination, which can impact on how they relate to others.

SEND Code of Practice p97

Communication is the act of transferring meaning or information from one individual to another or one medium to another. Language is one such 'carrier' we use to transfer this information. Interaction makes us realise that communication requires someone else to understand our communications.

In communicating with someone we need to have a reason or purpose to pass the "message" along, a composition of the message, a way to encode it, a way to transmit, a way to receive, the ability to decode and a way to interpret or make sense of the message. If at any point one of these mechanisms is impaired then the message will not be sent, received or interpreted correctly. Pupils with speech difficulties (dysfluency) may struggle with the transmission or composition of the message. Pupils with autistic spectrum conditions may fail to understand the reason or purpose of passing the message along or not have the 'code-breaking' instructions to understand the transmission. Whilst it is tempting to include pupils with a hearing impairment in here, since their need is defined medically rather than neurologically (in the brain), they are placed under sensory impairment instead.

The common C&I difficulties encountered in mainstream schools:

~ SLCN – (Speech, Language and Communication Needs) which covers any pupils with a stammer (dsyfluency), speech impediment, dysarthria (difficulty with mouth movements), delays with receptive and/or expressive language, selective mutism, auditory processing disorder (APD)
It is quite clear how the definition of communication can be applied to these difficulties.

~ ASC – (Autistic Spectrum Conditions, also called ASD Autistic Spectrum Disorders/Difficulties) which covers Autism, Asperger's, Social/(Semantic) Pragmatic Communication Disorder, PDA (Pathological Demand Avoidance), PDD (Pervasive Developmental Disorder) and ODD (Oppositional Defiance Disorder). Although the trend is to now call the difficulties experienced ASC, it can sometimes be useful to have the older terms since these came with quite clear distinctions. Asperger's is commonly called High functioning autism and pupils with this had average to high intelligence which often masked their other difficulties. Conversely, those with autism generally have lower intelligence scores and are often considered to have severe or profound and multiple learning difficulties. It is less obvious how these fit with the Communication and Interaction area of need until you consider that for a diagnosis of any of these the child must display ongoing difficulties with social communication and interaction. Until recently, it was the triad of impairments that had to be met for a diagnosis (Persistent difficulties with social interaction, persistent difficulties with social interaction, restricted and repetitive behaviours/activities/interests). This is now a dryad of impairments since the social and communication elements have been drawn into one criteria.

When entering assess information for these pupils you will be looking for observations, behaviour information, progress and attainment data and possibly cross-reference to checklists that indicate possible difficulties.

Our pupil has difficulties with social interactions, data gathered may include...

~ Speech and Language Therapy report on receptive and expressive language

~ Educational Psychology report with assessments and observations

~ Records of 'incidents'

~ CATS data

~ Anecdotal evidence from all sources of meltdowns and challenging situations

~ Information from the paediatrician

Social, Emotional and Mental Health (SEMH)
The SEND Code of Practice says:

6.32 Children and young people may experience a wide range of social and emotional difficulties which manifest themselves in many ways. These may include becoming withdrawn or isolated, as well as displaying challenging, disruptive or disturbing behaviour. These behaviours may reflect underlying mental health difficulties such as anxiety or depression, self-harming, substance misuse, eating disorders or physical symptoms that are medically unexplained. Other children and young people may have disorders such as attention deficit disorder, attention deficit hyperactive disorder or attachment disorder.

6.33 Schools and colleges should have clear processes to support children and young people, including how they will manage the effect of any disruptive behaviour so it does not adversely affect other pupils. The Department for Education publishes guidance on managing pupils' mental health and behaviour difficulties in schools – see the References section under Chapter 6 for a link.

SEND Code of Practice p98

The new Code of Practice replaced Behavioural, Emotional and Social Difficulties (BESD) with SEMH. This was done to reflect that behavioural needs are often manifestations of needs in other areas as opposed to a definable need of their own. Whilst in the section covering the Cognition and Learning broad area of need, you will have seen a caveat against ADHD/ADD. They were traditionally included under the BESD category and despite the definition of C&L being quite fitting, these conditions are included under SEMH.

This is the fastest growing area of need in schools and it is not difficult to see why with the increasing number of pupils identified as having mental health needs or eating disorders.

The common SEMH needs found in schools:

~ ADHD (Attention Deficit Hyperactivity Disorder), ADD (Attention Deficit Disorder) and Attachment Disorder which often exhibit with behavioural signs.

~ Anorexia, bulimia, depression, anxiety, school phobia, self-harm, substance and alcohol abuse which are often 'hidden' difficulties/disabilities.

~ Psychological difficulties such as schizophrenia, post-traumatic stress disorder (PTSD)and bipolar disorder

Pupils with ongoing medical difficulties (such as IBS or epilepsy) may experience emotional distresses which means their needs place them on the SEN register under this area of need. This would also include pupils with a cancer diagnosis or life-limiting illness.

Entering information in the assess section will involve looking at behaviour information, observations and the full range of academic information available. This is perhaps the most complex area to 'assess'. As a result you will have a lot of anecdotal information and opinions to work with and less empirical or numerical values.

Look for information from...

~ Educational psychology
~ Paediatrician/GP
~ CAMHS
~ Nurses/Hospital
~ Counsellor
~ Academic potential 'v' output.
~ Mentors

Sensory and Physical Difficulties (SPD)
The SEND Code of Practice says:

6.34 Some children and young people require special educational provision because they have a disability which prevents or hinders them from making use of the educational facilities generally provided. These difficulties can be age related and may fluctuate over time. Many children and young people with vision impairment (VI), hearing impairment (HI) or a multi-sensory impairment (MSI) will require specialist support and/or equipment to access their learning, or habilitation support. Children and young people with an MSI have a combination of vision and hearing difficulties. Information on how to provide services for deafblind children and young people is available through the Social Care for Deafblind Children and Adults guidance published by the Department of Health (see the References section under Chapter 6 for a link).

6.35 Some children and young people with a physical disability (PD) require additional ongoing support and equipment to access all the opportunities available to their peers.

SEND Code of Practice p98

Sensory difficulties are medically diagnosed. They are not a result of neurological (brain related) problems. So, conditions such as APD (auditory processing disorder) which are due to the brain processing the information rather than a defect in the hearing organs belongs under C&I not SPD. This is the least represented category in mainstream schools often due to the very different approaches and adaptations needed to teach the children involved.

Physical difficulties can be catered for in most schools since the Disability Discrimination Act/Equalities Act and the Disability Access Plan that each school has to produce should have made pre-emptive adaptations to the environment for pupils with physical abilities to attend. Whilst for many of us the phrase physical difficulty conjures up images of wheelchairs, it may also include walking sticks, pupils who manage without any physical aids but who need more space or lifts for moving around the building. Disabled access toilets, often with hoists and showering facilities should be available and the whole school aesthetic considered in relation to the pupils it houses (including tactile surfaces, acoustics and paint scheme indicating floors, walls and gradient changes.

The common SPD in schools:

~ Hearing Impairment (HI) – The difficulties here could range from minor hearing loss (either from birth or later in life) through to complete hearing loss. Pupils may be able to manage with a modified environment, hearing aids and radio aids or may need sign supported English or full BSL. It is worth bearing in mind that communication is 2-way. So, just providing a translation of your lessons is not enough, pupils need a way to communicate back to you. They also need a way to communicate with their peers or will become isolated.

~ Visual Impairment (VI) – Again the range of difficulties is wide. Some pupils need a strong visual prescription, others wouldn't benefit from prescriptive lenses and magnifiers or CCTV is needed. At the far extreme of the spectrum a pupil may be registered blind. They may need to learn braille both for reading and writing and there will be difficulties with mobility around the school site necessitating the use of buddies, white sticks and possibly guide-dogs.

~ Multi-sensory Impairment (MSI) – It would be unusual to find a pupil with complete multi-sensory impairment in a mainstream school.

~ Physical Disabilities are wide ranging and not always obvious. All physical abilities are driven by a medical need, and although not every pupil labelled with that need will be on the SEN register, they do have protected characteristics in law and you want to ensure their needs are being met.

~   Visible **PD**: Cerebral Palsy, Motor Neurone Disease, Hemiplegia, Multiple Sclerosis, Scoliosis, Restricted Growth, Spina Bifida, Muscular Dystrophy

~   Invisible **PD**: Cystic Fibrosis, Heart Disease, Juvenile Rheumatoid Arthritis, Sickle Cell Anaemia

Much of your assess information will come from the pupil, parents and professionals. Their needs may impact on the academic achievement and so this will need to be considered too.

What about all the others?

There are some needs that just don't seem to fit under a single heading. Where do we put a child with Fragile X Syndrome or Foetal Alcohol Syndrome?

The answer is not simple and some schools will categorise differently. My rule of thumb was always to look at where their needs lie and the support I am providing since this is the definition of SEN-ness in the SEN Code of Practice. If they are struggling academically with literacy skills then they need to go under Cognition and Learning as their primary area of need. If the majority of their need is focussed around social interaction then they go under the Communication and Interaction section. I can then add as many additional areas as necessary to reflect their secondary areas of need.

Here is as good a place as any to mention **English as an Additional Language**. The lack of English is not in itself sufficient reason to add a pupil to the SEN Register. Despite the fact a pupil may be accessing interventions they are accessing them to develop their English skills. If, however, they display difficulties in their first language, or after a couple of years of immersive English teaching they are not making expected progress with skills and English acquisition then it would be prudent to consider whether there are underlying SEN issues.

The SEN Code of Practice says:

5.30 Practitioners should look carefully at all aspects of a child's learning and development to establish whether any delay is related to learning English as an additional language or if it arises from SEN or disability. Difficulties related solely to learning English as an additional language are not SEN.

This does not prevent you using a version of the graduated approach to record what you are doing with these pupils to help them further develop their English skills, but take care to make your work distinct from your SEN obligations and ensure staff in your school also do the same.

Assessment Complete:
If you have worked your way through this chapter, the you should have a good understanding of the 'assess' part of the graduated response. You will know some of the sources of data you might wish to use, know that it may need 'interpreting', and if you choose to use a Learning Plan, you will know where you can enter the 'assess' information.

I have introduced the Areas of Need and given a brief overview of each. On the next page are bookmarks useful for NQTS, RQTS and staff in general to understand the areas of need. In my school, I used to add our top-tips to the back of each one. If we had a new member of staff arrive partway through the year, or only a handful of NQTs/RQTs I would attach a list of pupils they would be teaching for whom the bookmark was relevant. An alternative, is to add an 'initial checklist' to the back of each bookmark to enable staff to identify pupils who may fall under the broad areas of need identified. Or perhaps you would like to list the subcategories in your school relevant to each bookmark.

Bookmarks

Cognition & Learning (C&L)	Communication & Interaction (C&I)
Pupils display difficulties across all areas of the curriculum. They need support with any classroom activities that will involve: knowledge, attention, memory and working memory, judgment and evaluation, reasoning and computation, problem solving and decision making, comprehension and production of language.	Pupils demonstrate difficulty in understanding communication or interacting appropriately. Sometimes their difficulties are well hidden behind an expansive vocabulary or copying the behaviours of other in the class.
Reasonable adjustments:	**Reasonable adjustments**:
Opportunities for overlearning (don't rush through topics of work.)	Clear instructions with visual cues.
Break tasks into small chunks.	Collaborative working although this may need mediation
Use alternative methods of recording.	Time given to organise and verbalise ideas and responses
Make links to prior learning explicit.	Uncluttered, clearly organised classroom environment
	Modification of timetable to reflect needs

Social, Emotional & Mental Health (SEMH)	Sensory & Physical Difficulties (SPD)
Pupils may not show outward signs of their difficulties. Behaviour is often a manifestation of an underlying problem. A pupil's mental health is likely to impact on their learning regardless of ability.	Pupils with sensory difficulties may not be immediately obvious and not all pupils with physical difficulties may stand out. Many hidden physical difficulties have serious underlying health implications.
Reasonable adjustments:	**Reasonable adjustments**:
Time out and calming activities	Reconsider seating arrangements and adjust according to activities
Fiddle toys or acceptable 'distraction' techniques (doodling)	Adaptation of books, worksheets, slides
Be aware of the side effects of any medication	Use of physical aids and adapted equipment
Address the underlying problem not the observable behaviour	Time out for breaks
Modification of behaviour rules to reflect needs	Catch up work for absences (work packs for planned absences)
	Modification of uniform rules to reflect needs

Planning

There is now more flexibility for schools to record support, outcomes and progression in a way that they think would most benefit pupils. It is important to note that as part of any inspection, OFSTED will expect to see evidence of learner progress, a focus on outcomes and a rigorous approach to the monitoring and evaluation of any SEN support provided.

So, once we have all the 'assess' information about our pupil it is time to look at addressing the areas of difficulty we have identified. This is our 'action plan' and is where old Individual Education Plans were helpful, but Passports or Person-Centred Plans can achieve the same goals. We are identifying what we need to achieve and how we are planning to do so. In the tradition of action planning we are going to include SMART targets. Tempting though it is to identify and deliver school based targets, we need to involve the parents and child in developing them. A buy-in from all parties will generally ensure greater success and when parents are involved you can get them on board with supporting. A passport can be great at getting children to express their 'voice' – what do they think they can contribute to help develop further. This becomes more important as they get older and we develop their independence and self-advocacy skills.

The SEN Code of Practice says:

6.48 Where it is decided to provide a pupil with SEN support, the parents must be formally notified, although parents should have already been involved in forming the assessment of needs as outlined. The teacher and the SENCO should agree in consultation with the parent and the pupil the adjustments, interventions and support to be put in place, as well as the expected impact on progress, development or behaviour, along with a clear date for review.

6.49 All teachers and support staff who work with the pupil should be made aware of their needs, the outcomes sought, the support provided and any teaching strategies or approaches that are required. This should also be recorded on the school's information system.

6.50 The support and intervention provided should be selected to meet the outcomes identified for the pupil, based on reliable evidence of effectiveness, and should be provided by staff with sufficient skills and knowledge.

6.51 Parents should be fully aware of the planned support and interventions and, where appropriate, plans should seek parental involvement to reinforce or contribute to progress at home. The information set out in 6.39 should be readily available to and discussed with the pupil's parents.

So, we are required to formalise a plan of action and although the SEN Code of Practice doesn't state how to do this (it says a short note in the child's records will do) it does imply a 'plan' will be created.

Our record for the pupil needs to identify what we are going to change (differentiation and environment), what provisions we might use and what support will be put in place along with what we 'think' the results/outcomes will be with a clear idea of how long it will take to reach that outcome. This record then needs to be shared with everyone who works with the pupil.

I would be surprised if you are unfamiliar with the concept of SMART target setting, however, familiarity doesn't always make us very good at it! I'll admit to struggling at times and sometimes we need to put another pair of eyes over it and come up with something suitable.

Let's consider the different elements and then see how they feed into the program to allow us to set targets for our pupils.

SMART, once stood for Specific, Measurable, Achievable, Realistic and Time-bound, but over the years education has begun to borrow alternative interpretations from the world of business. Which 'phrase' you choose to complete the acronym is up to you but they all result in high quality targets.

Columbo was SMART

Specific	Significant, Stretching	What do we want to achieve? (Be exact, make it important and let it extend the current level)
Measurable	Meaningful, Motivating	How do we track progress and measure the result of a goal that has a purpose and therefore an inspiration for us and for the pupil?
Achievable	Agreed upon, Attainable, Acceptable, Action-oriented	The goal needs to be agreed with everyone involved as sensible, suitable at this point, likely to be successful, and contributable towards future success.
Realistic	Relevant, Reasonable, Rewarding, Results-oriented	Is the goal within reach, useful and of value?
Time-bound	Time-based, Timely, Tangible, Trackable	Is there a deadline or milestone against which to measure the progress made?

The alternative approach is the Columbo strategy: 6Ws + H + E. This involves asking a series of questions; who, what, when, where, which, why, how and explain.

S	Who needs to be involved? What needs to be accomplished/ When by (overall)? Where does this need to take place? Which obstacles may block our path? Why do we need this goal?
M	How will we measure success? How do we know we have been successful?
A	Explain if we have the skills needed Explain the motivation behind the goal Explain the effort needed
R	Why set this now?
T	What is the deadline?

Molly Candy is my hypothetical pupil. I wrote out her strengths and concerns earlier. She has MLD and VI and our assessments indicated that she was a strong auditory learner. We suggested she needed to work on her reading skills as she is 3 years behind where we would expect her to be.

I know that the reference to reading age was based on a comprehension test – so this is where I need to focus support/intervention. I also know that she can 'read' single words without a problem, it is her general exposure to and understanding of whole texts that needs development rather than her ability to 'decode' phonics.

If I was to type a target for Molly it would probably read:

Molly needs to improve her reading comprehension skills as measured using the Literacy Assessment Online reading test in 3 months' time, with an expected increase from a standard score of 75 to 82 by accessing a graduated reading program using the Dockside books from stage 3 and the accompanying exercises. Molly will be able to read the books at home and discuss the content with her parents who can use the questions in the back of the books to engage Molly in a general comprehension discussion, whilst in school she will attend a 10-minute reading session in the library at 8:40am every morning for a 1:1 session with the librarian where they will work through the teacher guided activities. Molly should not speed through the books but should spend at least 3 days with each one. This will be reviewed in 3-months.

Well there's plenty of information there, but no-one is going to read it and far fewer will do anything with it! It would be better set out in an accessible table. You could use a word-processed document, a Spreadsheet or a commercial program to achieve this.

Area of Concern	Target	Desired Outcome	Strategies & Provision	Key Staff
Comprehension	To improve reading comprehension skills (measure on LAO)	Standard score will increase from 75 to 82 in 3 months	Dockside reading books stage 3. Reading at home and oral answers to questions. 1:1 time with librarian (8:40am daily) on teacher guided activities.	Librarian Parents

I now have a target for Molly that clearly indicates all the aspects I need. This format is much more 'readable' especially for busy school staff you need to inform.

I added two more two targets which might also be appropriate.

Comprehension	To read at home for 5 minutes every day.	Observed on 10 occasions. Will contribute to the improved LAO score.	Daily reading record, reward system, opportunities for demonstrating progress, graded reading ability books.	Parents
VI (Visual impairment)	Molly says she will wear spectacles as prescribed.	Observed by Learning Support Assistant/teachers and eventually done without prompting.	Learning Support Assistant to remind pupil to wear spectacles when necessary.	All relevant TAs Pupil

(Screen shots from Edukey's Learning Plans and Provision Maps.)

Now, my next comment comes with a health warning…do not enter too many targets! If you have any pupils with EHCPs you are going to need to break down those 'whole-stage' goals into smaller termly achievable targets, but you will see there are far too many of them. Focus on 3-5 and you are likely to see impact and be able to move onto new targets, rather than spreading yourself (and the pupil) too thin. For pupils on your SEN Support 3-5 targets is about right for a classroom/subject teacher and the pupil themselves to focus on. This may mean you have to review more frequently, but there is no harm in that.

Of course, the targets will all boil down to the interventions/provisions you are putting in place. Remember that definition of SEN? The one that said they need to be accessing something different from/additional to? Our identified needs (from the assessment process) drive the interventions that are put in place which in turn drive the targets/goals which we set.

But a plan isn't just about what we want a pupil to achieve it is about the support (other than interventions/provisions) that we will put in place. Some of this will be reminders about the classroom environment and adaptations we need to accommodate.

A class teacher may just decide to add these directly to their scheme of work to show how it is adapted to meet the needs of pupils in the class. Whilst this is very helpful, as a SENDCO it isn't always incredibly useful unless we have access to all the schemes of work. Put quite simply, when, as a SENDCO, we are sat in a challenging meeting we need to know exactly what has been in place for a pupil.

If there is anything else someone needs to know about the pupil it is useful to include on their plan. I use a summary box, in this case to remind staff about Molly's visual difficulties.

Summary
To help with Molly's visual difficulties:
Use Green paper with size 16pt bold font for ALL printed material.
Where possible use a pale green background for overhead slides and avoid cluttered slides/worksheets.
Keep a well-lit classroom and consider carefully where Molly sits.
Allow her to use her wedge to bring work closer to her line of vision rather than hunching over her work.
Give Molly verbal cues and reminders as she will not pick up on non-verbal signals.

Do not ask Molly to copy chunks of text from books or the board - she is unable to switch her focus between two sources easily. Encourage Molly to wear her glasses.

We mustn't forget the parent and pupil contributions. Some of these will be concluded in the strength and difficulties already written up, but if there is anything else they want to say, a record is useful.

Parents
Molly's parents are keen that she should access a broad curriculum. They would like her to take responsibility for her own organisation. They will take Molly for a new eye-test
Pupil
I'm looking forward to my new school. I know I need to wear my glasses and I'll try to remember them.
SENDCO
Whilst Molly's previous school had her on their SEN register and provided the above verbal information they were unable to provide any assessments. Our school will engage the local authority visual impairment team for additional advice and assessment (request sent 1.4.18) and undertake diagnostic assessments to establish the level of Molly's needs. This plan should be seen as temporary to meet Molly's immediate needs.
Additional Information
Up-to-date reading and spelling assessment (intake tests - LAO) [SS 75 on 1.4.18]. CAT4 tests (all pupils do these on intake) [Booked 4.4.18]. 1:1 assessment of Molly's comprehension skills - WIATT-ii (T) [Booked 5.4.18]. WRIT assessment [Booked 3.4.18]. Visual Impairment team and relevant assessments.

Map it

Provision mapping is a transparent model of showing the range of provision available to learners throughout the school it allows schools to monitor, evaluate and plan the development of provision, increase access for disadvantaged groups, secure the entitlement of all learners and raise achievement and standards. An effective provision map gives a clear link between provision and learner progress.

Traditionally the planning for pupils and the provisions put in place were two separate ideas. Sometimes, usually by luck, the targets on the plan matched the outcomes of the interventions. What was happening was a plan which identified our pupil need support with spelling saw them entered into a spelling intervention...but that intervention wasn't necessarily targeting the spellings that our pupil needed support with. Now, with the pressure on to develop in-class intervention, the provisions tend to be far more tailored to the individual. Our pupil struggling with spelling words with the 'ed' ending will be targeted with provision that supports development of 'ed' endings. Therefore, when the progress is measured, it is not only against the outcomes of the intervention but also the specific required outcomes for the pupil...two birds with one stone! (That's not to say it's any easier though!)

Doing

I love the 'do' part of the graduated response (I think I'll always embrace the traditional SEN-Do part of the role over the SEN-Co elements!). This is the part where we get on and 'do' what we have said we will in the plan. It's where we translate the targets into actions. This part is also the defining part of SEN: Remember that definition? A child is SEN if they are in receipt of support which is additional to/different from other pupils in the school. The recording of this has generally been replaced by a provision map where the costs, frequency and a whole host of further information is kept.

This is where, I take my hat off to the original Edukey planning team when they developed their program Learning Plans and Provision Maps. They separated the provisions section from the planning section, which at the time confused me – however, what it means is, I can set up all the interventions/provisions in my school and have them automatically feed into each individual child's plan. If I open up a plan and there are no interventions/provisions there – what is this telling me? (Either I've not set something up, or the child isn't actually SEN!) I don't need to have their program for that though. I can look at my information and if I'm not 'doing' something then I seriously need to question if the pupil belongs on the SEN register or whether I need to put something in place.

Let's have a closer look at the idea of 'doing' something.

The SEN Code of Practice says:

6.52 The class or subject teacher should remain responsible for working with the child on a daily basis. Where the interventions involve group or one-to-one teaching away from the main class or subject teacher, they should still retain responsibility for the pupil. They should work closely with any teaching assistants or specialist staff involved, to plan and assess the impact of support and interventions and how they can be linked to classroom teaching. The SENCO should support the class or subject teacher in the further assessment of the child's particular strengths and weaknesses, in problem solving and advising on the effective implementation of support.

I know from experience that in primary schools the class teachers take a far more active role in identifying and implementing interventions for pupils on the SEN register, then their counterparts in secondary schools where the onus appears to be upon the SENDCO (and team) to identify, plan and deliver. However, the SEN Code of Practice is very clear that class and subject teachers should take responsibility for interventions run away from their classrooms.

How can we make this work?

The doing element happens in two places, during lessons (preferable) and during withdrawal groups (realistic and for certain interventions more appropriate). Instantly we can see that if it is happening during a lesson there is more opportunity for the teacher to input, monitor and even deliver, linking the intervention to the whole class exercises. In a primary classroom this could take the form of a highly structured and differentiated activity using the theme of the main session but explicitly teaching related to their targets.

In a secondary this is not impossible but may be more difficult. Again, it could take the form of quality differentiation, providing an activity targeted at the identified need, or it might be an agreed approach/marking focus for most departments with one taking responsibility for 'teaching' the skill and others providing application opportunities.

Realistically in a secondary a focused intervention on spelling or reading, for example, is more likely to take place outside the classroom. The teachers may not have oversight of these provisions and a simple feedback/information system is needed. You could ask their regular Maths or English teacher to input into relevant provisions – perhaps by suggesting a text they could use, or by informing the intervention team what the topic is being covered in class so that the interventions can be tailored to link to the classroom experience. If you are using a purchased scheme of intervention (such as Ruth Miskin Fresh Start) this can be slightly more difficult to achieve, so it may be a two-way exchange and the usual English teacher perhaps feeds some of the work from the intervention into their lesson rather than the other way around. Just knowing which phonic sound you've worked on this week can allow them to feed it into words they use in class and look out for opportunities to positively mark their work for independent use of the sound.

6.75 As outlined in 'Involving parents and pupils in planning and reviewing progress' from paragraph 6.63, the school should readily share this information with parents. It should be provided in a format that is accessible (for example, a note setting out the areas of discussion following a regular SEN support meeting or tracking data showing the pupil's progress together with highlighted sections of a provision map that enables parents to see the support that has been provided).

When we share the action plan with the parents (and young person) we need to tell them how we are going to meet their needs. A list of interventions/provisions at this stage can be useful. It is worth noting at this point that the best provisions use the data from your original assessments as this then feeds back into whether or not the interventions are successful but also if the targets you have set the pupils are suitable. The information provided does not need to be prescriptive but something more than just a title can be helpful to avoid ambiguity or misunderstanding of what you mean.

6.76 Provision maps are an efficient way of showing all the provision that the school makes which is additional to and different from that which is offered through the school's curriculum. The use of provision maps can help SENCOs to maintain an overview of the programmes and interventions used with different groups of pupils and provide a basis for monitoring the levels of intervention.

On the whole school level, a provision map can tell you where all your resources are focused, or need to be focused and if you track the finances too it can help you make informed decisions about future work. I love a good provision map and I've seen many versions, each adapted to the needs of the school and the individuals using them.

For example, a class teacher needs to know what interventions and when (almost a timetable) but they don't need costs. A TA who works

across several groups may need to know who, when and where. The SLT are more interested in how much!

6.77 Provision management can be used strategically to develop special educational provision to match the assessed needs of pupils across the school, and to evaluate the impact of that provision on pupil progress. Used in this way provision management can also contribute to school improvement by identifying particular patterns of need and potential areas of development for teaching staff. It can help the school to develop the use of interventions that are effective and to remove those that are less so. It can support schools to improve their core offer for all pupils as the most effective approaches are adopted more widely across the school.

Provision management is what you 'do' with your provision map! Many a school has a pretty map on the wall with a list of names (beware GDPR!), but it is what you do with the information beyond this that is the management element.

Plan to do

Here is a small part of my 'pretty' wall map from the beginning of my incursion into provision mapping – it was large and displayed prominently on the wall of my office for a whole 4 months before it dawned on me I needed to do something with it and that no-one ever looked at it expect me!

		Cognition and Learning	Communication and Interaction
Transition		Visits to primary schools re guidance and welfare New intake evening Student induction days in Summer term Open evening SENCO (or appropriate other) transition team arrange travel training Sensory team arrange travel training and visits SEN induction/transition day in Summer term TA working in primary	
KS3 KS3 only]	Wave 1 All students	Differentiated curriculum planning; activities; delivery and outcome Increased visual aids/modeling Visual timetables Alternative dictionaries Use of writing frames Access to ICT Clubs (including homework, library etc)	Differentiated curriculum planning; activities; delivery and outcome Increased visual aids/modelling Visual timetables Simplified language and key words Structured school and class routines
	Wave 2 Some students (usually SA)	Catch up programmes In-class support from TA Multi-sensory spelling groups Paired reading Student information to staff (passports) Time limited, targeted, intervention groups	Social skills group training Use of symbols In class support with focus on supporting speech and language Communication skills Social stories Comic strip conversations
	Wave 3 Few students (usually SAP)	Intense literacy/numeracy support Specialist teaching	Speech and language advice /support from autism and SALT Specialist teaching Whole school INSET
KS4 ppropriate provision from KS3	Wave 1 All students	Exam booster classes Revision classes	Revision classes
	Wave 2 Some students (usually SA)	Reduced/increasingly personalised timetable Guided Options choices Modified Curriculum/Basic skills	Guided Options choices Modified Curriculum
	Wave 3	Exam concessions	Speech and language advice /support from autism and SALT

Actually, it is more of a menu of what was available at the time, 'my school local offer'.

I'm pleased to say, that little gem is stored in the archived files box.

There are many books on the market dedicated to setting up provision maps. There are software solutions and there are courses you can go on. At the end of the day, you know what will work for you and how much information you want to include.

My approach is presented here, you are welcome to pinch ideas (isn't that why you have the book?). I also recommend (should you want more/alternative/advanced ideas) Anne Massey's Provision Mapping and the SEND Code of Practice.

Title	Description	Intended Outcome		
1:1 Dockside Comprehension	10 minutes each morning with Librarian. Work steadily through nominated stage of Dockside series. Complete Teacher guided activities with Librarian. Complete oral comprehension work with parents. Minimum 3 days with each book.	Pupils will improve their general comprehension skills. LAO used as baseline and re-test. 3 month's time scale (1 term) recommended. Scaling RAG. RED will indicate little or no improvement in standard scores. AMBER will indicate some improvement in standard scores. GREEN will indicate more than expected improvement in standard scores. It would be reasonable to expect a movement of 10 points in the standard score over a term in order to define 'progress'.		
Area of Need	**Wave**	**Start Date**	**End Date**	**Session length**
Cognition and Learning (Comprehension)	3 (Targeted)	16th April 2018	20th July 2018	10-minute sessions
Fixed costs	**Per pupil costs**	**Per session Costs**	**Other costs**	**Session frequency**
£84.93	£3.71	2.00	0.00	Daily (individually agreed times)
Total Cost	**Cost per pupil**	**Other information**		
516.06	172.09	Intervention is delivered 1:1 over 70 10-minute daily sessions		
Who will deliver	**Ratio of support**			
Librarian	1:1			
Who is in this intervention?	**Group**	**Baseline data**	**Outcomes**	**Notes**
Molly Candy Mandy Candy Milly Candy	Y11b Y11a Y11c	75 62 68		Green Overlay N/A

This is Molly's Dockside intervention set up, we all know she was one of triplets and all three of them have comprehension difficulties so have been included in this intervention!

You can include as much, or as little, detail as you want. Personally, I find it helpful to define what my baseline test is (and what I will use for measuring outcomes at the end) and what 'progress' actually looks like. You can use any scale you like for measuring progress, but it's helpful to think about what really poor progress, acceptable progress and exceptional progress would look like. For this example, I've only defined the extremes. You can identify a start and end date but also a mid-point check although I prefer to do that at my convenience so I've not included it on my grid.)

It is so important in our current financial climate to accurately record how much interventions/provisions are costing. Whilst a class teacher may not be involved in this, I'm afraid as SENDCO you don't have much choice but to grab a calculator and start crunching finances.

I've included overall costs in the table above, but I do find it helpful to almost create a receipt of each element (I use sticky-notes on my PC and then screen shot and save in a OneNote folder, but you could create a Document, Spreadsheet, use features of SEN programs or your MIS or even download a free invoicing program if you fancy being...fancy! Zoho Invoice is free to use, just avoid falling foul of GDPR and don't use pupil data or names.)

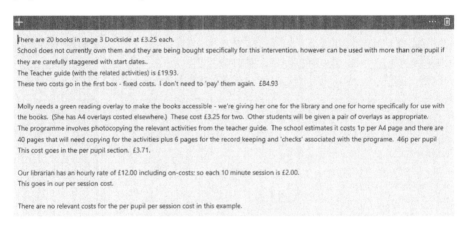

(Here is a screen post-it© with a breakdown of costs)

It's important we know what kinds of costs we are working with. You may discover a cross-over with Pupil Premium cohorts at this point. You may prefer to keep your provision maps totally separate. Mine had so

much overlap it would have been an unnecessary duplication of work to create as separate maps.

Fixed Costs	Per Pupil Costs	Per Session Costs	Per Pupil Per Session
Anything you can generally re-use after the first intervention, which means you need to be careful you only account for their cost once! It also includes returnable items.	These are anything a pupil takes away or uses that you need to replace.	This box can be used to record a rate of pay for any adults involved or the cost of hiring a room.	This is not usually completed if the previous two boxes are filled in. Often used for LAC where they have selected an activity that involves taking a buddy.
A Teacher Guide A set of books (reusable) A box of Lego iPads/Laptops/ Dictaphone The cost of training staff to deliver the intervention (including cover) Licence fees A classroom resource box of fidget toys, pencil grips, dyslexia friendly resources. Writing wedge Weighted cushions Noisy balls	Write-in workbooks Overlays Pencil grips Fidget toys Photocopying/lamin ating of resources Set of school uniform Individual licence fees Assessment costs	Per session rate of pay for staff (especially external staff) Per session rate for room hire	Peripatetic sessions (music, swimming) Breakfast/after-school club Examination concessions (reader/scribe if paid) Horse-riding sessions with a buddy (LAC – yes, this is real and was approved by the virtual head, as was rock climbing the following year)

Alternatively, some schools record costs under the headings: Stationery, Equipment, Books, People/Location, Other. Some will just allocate a total cost without any breakdown. It depends on what works for you.

As a couple of worked examples:

We decide to train a member of the TA team in precision teaching in order to run an intervention with 4 children on a 1:1 basis over the next half term (which has 35 working days). There is a course on offer at the local authority at as cost of £125. To cover the staff member for the day will cost £90. There is a book/guide recommended which costs £23.99. A website is used to generate the precision teaching worksheets – it's free to use, but we need to print 1 worksheet per child, per week. We decided not to laminate the sheets but placed them in spare plastic wallets instead. All the children had appropriate overlays from other sessions. Our TA hourly rate with on costs is £18/hour and she will deliver the intervention in 15-minute blocks every school day. The next time I run this intervention I won't need to enter the fixed costs...unless we've lost the guidebook or it's a different member of staff who needs training.

Fixed Costs	Per Pupil Costs	Per Session Costs	Per Pupil Per Session
Training £125 Cover £90 Guide book £23.99 TOTAL £238.99	7p (our school charges 1p per A4 B&W photocopy and we need 1 sheet per child per week) Yes, this is a ridiculously small amount...until you realise that 100 pupils in 10 interventions soon adds up!)	TA - £18/4 = £4.50 (15 minute-session)	Not relevant

We decided to employ an external speech and language therapist to work with a small group (6) of pupils who have similar needs. He was contracted for 6-8 sessions and we agreed a set rate per session, regardless of how many pupils attended. The therapist bought his own resources. We agreed that if a session was cancelled through his illness/unavailability to attend then we would not be charged.

At the end of the time period we can calculate total cost based on the number of sessions that took place.

Fixed Costs	Per Pupil Costs	Per Session Costs	Per Pupil Per Session
		£37.50	

Two of our pupils have a hearing impairment and despite using lip-reading in the majority of their lessons where they know the staff they both prefer to use BSL when working with external providers. We have a careers event next term and they have requested BSL support for the externally led sessions. There are 8 externally led sessions for each pupil over the course of the week. A BSL specialist lives locally and is known to the pupils, the specialist has agreed to attend for just the sessions they need their support (rather than us having to pay a full day rate each day.) The specialist has also agreed that if the pupils feel comfortable to access the sessions without her support towards the end of the week then we can cancel. Her rate per session is £26.75. The two pupils have chosen different workshops so she could be attending up to 16 times. We need to wait until the end before we can calculate a total final cost.

Fixed Costs	Per Pupil Costs	Per Session Costs	Per Pupil Per Session
			£26.75

By entering the figures into the correct columns of the table we can start to build up a very accurate picture of our spending for each pupil, and in our current climate of ever decreasing budgets this is essential.

This is all well and good for an intervention of provision going on outside the classroom or with another member of staff during a specified activity – but how can we make class teachers and subject teachers more involved and taking responsibility?

First of all, they should be contributing their own additions to the provision map, you might need to make it look 'pretty' and uniform (unless you're happy to record in a variety of ways – it would drive me nuts!) but they should be able to tell you what they are doing. Your headings might need a little tweaking.

Let's suggest that Molly Candy is having difficulty with understanding and using spelling rules for plurals. All of her teachers have picked up on it and both the English and humanities department have suggested they can support. Her target is written onto her plan (or whatever you are using to communicate her needs across the school). The provision put in place is for the English department to explicitly teach pluralisation rules over the course of the next 6 weeks and share what they are teaching and when with her humanities teacher via email. Week one they are going to focus on words ending with 'x'. So, the humanities teacher builds in opportunities for Molly to use words ending in x and their plural to their lessons, giving her feedback and reminding her how the English department have introduced the rule. This is brilliant joined-up work but it's how we record this is what is happening is the tricky part.

Title	Description		Intended Outcome		
English/ Humanity Spelling support	English and humanities departments work together to address spelling difficulties for a variety of pupils. Targets tend to be bespoke for each pupil. English will teach explicitly (approx. 5 minutes every lesson) Humanities will give opportunities to apply verbally or in writing.		Pupils will improve their general spelling skills and specific spelling skills to their area of weakness. See identified targets below. Molly – To spell plurals Milly – To spell words with the long /a/ phoneme Many – To spell words with an 'ed' ending.		
Area of Need	Wave	Start Date	End Date	Session length	
Cognition and Learning (Comprehension)	2 (In-class)	16th April 2018	20th July 2018	5-minutes + application	
Fixed costs	Per pupil costs	Per session Costs	Other costs	Session frequency	
			No costs	Every English lesson (5x weekly). All humanities lessons 3x weekly	
Total Cost	Cost per pupil	Other information			

		Intervention is delivered by class teachers as part of class teaching and beneficial to all pupils OR delivered as a targeted piece of work within class by teacher/TA		
Who will deliver	*Ratio of support*			
English/Humanities	1:1 or 1:30			
Who is in this intervention?	*Group*	*Baseline data*	*Outcomes*	*Notes*
Molly Candy	Y11b	1/10 words correctly pluralised	*(I can fill this in at the end of the intervention)*	Green Overlay
Mandy Candy	Y11a	0/10 words ending in /ed/ correct		N/A
Milly Candy	Y11c	2/10 long /a/ phonemes correct		N/A

Now, I feel a little more confident walking into a SEN review for Molly knowing exactly what provisions she is getting and how her needs are being addressed in every lesson.

I'm a realist though. I know that in a lot of schools asking the class/subject teachers to work this way is likely to be a challenge! If they did work this way for all of the children we identify with SEN and they did have the time (reduced workload) to record for us what they are doing to support each one, then we would be out of a job (which of course is our personal aim anyway in achieving full integration for our pupils) and SEN'ness as such wouldn't exist.

We need to find a compromise.

I've seen many models and I've seen many SENDCOs, me included, pull out their hair in frustration. One of the best models I've seen simply asks teachers to annotate their long term/medium term plans with how they will meet additional needs in their classroom (at both ends of the spectrum.) They don't have to be detailed and they probably won't link to the individual pupil targets (☹) but at least we would be on the right tracks. The alternative is an overview sheet. What are the barriers? What we will do to address the targets and outcomes? (Blank copies of both attached in the appendix.) Whatever model is chosen it is essential that outcomes are central to their development and reporting.

Teacher		Group	Subject		Any additional support? Used for?
Mr Hertz		11Sc3A	Science. Next unit is genetics.		2/3 sessions. Practical support for VI.
Date From		*Date To*			
16th April		20th July			
Who	*Barriers*	*Targets*	*What I'll do*	*Resources*	*Baseline*	*Outcome*
Mo Ca	Spelling VI	Plurals	Focus in next unit	Green paper	1/10	7/10
Ma Ca	Spelling	'ed' words	One word each lesson		0/10	50/10
Mi Ca	Spelling	/a/ sound	Identify each lesson		2/10	10/10

Gone are the days of lesson plans for every lesson (well, they have in most schools and for most staff, although everywhere is different and some staff can expect to have to produce detailed lesson plans: e.g training teachers.) However, subjects and departments have medium- and long-term plans which can serve as useful recording documents.

Ideally, planning for pupil needs can take place when the plans are initially created, pre-empting difficulties and making suggestions which are then tweaked to individual needs. Where the ideal doesn't exist, or a new need becomes apparent, an annotated plan with any changes would be helpful.

Sadly, these plans don't address the outcomes for specific pupils and you need to rely on data collected from other sources.

Whilst both these models are fine, just bear in mind that as SENDCO you've got to extract the information from them to make it useful in reporting SEN pupil progress both generally and in addressing their difficulties. They will both involve chasing down a number of staff several times a year to gather the information (and we know some will

be better at providing it than others who will have forgotten to do their annotations after week 1!)

Title		Year	Subject	Topic
Inheritance, Variation & Reproduction (Variation & Evolution)		11	Science	Genetics
Session	**Objectives**	**Delivery**		**Modification**
1	Define the term extinction. Explain how extinction may be caused. Explain that organisms become extinct because something changes and the species cannot adapt quickly enough to the new circumstances.	Give a list of extinct organisms and ask pupils to print images. Suggest reasons to explain why they died out. Produce a poster of pictures of extinct organisms. Discuss the evidence we have that they looked like this. Explain why some organisms are endangered. Give examples. Give reasons why it is important to prevent species from becoming extinct. Research causes of extinction and write a report/ PowerPoint presentation to present to the class.		Ensure key vocabulary is provided Produce a 'dictionary'/'glossary' Label display Choose activity *Remind pupils of spelling targets and suggest words they could use MoCa – dinosaur, organism, species, flying fox, black-tailed mouse MaCa – died, prevented, endangered, looked MiCa – explain, whale, snail, black-tailed mouse*
2				

Do the do

Once we've got accurate figures and we know who needs the intervention, when we are delivering it, what the outcomes will be, who will facilitate the delivery and bought any resources to deliver it, we then need to 'get on with the task'.

Whilst we have usually set an end review date it is worth recalling that we can, and should, review at any time. A check after the first few sessions is essential if we are to be sure we have made the right decision about our intervention package for each individual we have placed in there. This is especially true if there is an expensive commercial resource you've bought in rather than using bespoke, homespun approaches.

One of the hardest jobs as a SENDCO is challenging our colleagues! It is highly likely, these days, that you are not the person implementing any intervention. It may fall to departments (the Maths and English team are commonly used), class teachers (in primary schools), staff with 'capacity' (in secondary schools) or your own TA team. Your job as co-ordinator is to check on the provisions in place for each individual and where appropriate intervene or challenge. To do that, you need to be clear what the provision is for and what outcomes are expected.

In my training sessions, I often share the story of when I first started using Learning Plans and Provision Maps (many years ago!). All my TAs had their own 'reading' group where they were delivering sessions designed to improve the reading age of pupils. I made two mistakes a) leaving them to it, and b) not being specific in the expected outcomes. My TAs evaluated/reviewed the interventions at the end of the cycle and all the pupils appeared to have done very well. The only problem was, as the class teacher for many of them I knew they hadn't made progress with their reading ages. A quick reading test confirmed my fears. Many of the pupils had stayed the same if not gone backwards! A most uncomfortable staff meeting followed. I accepted that I should have been checking on the intervention regularly and providing feedback to the staff (and pupils) involved. We also realised that the outcomes they measured were not the outcomes of the provision. My TAs had given the pupils excellent ratings because they were attending their sessions (it was held as a breakfast club), taking part, eating the toast/biscuits, engaging with the TAs in general conversation and not because they had read the books/words, completed the games/activities or made progress with their reading skills. If we had adjusted the provision to be one measuring their social interactions skills, attendance and engagement progress then my TAs were not wrong with their judgements – unfortunately this was a reading intervention! I suppose I'm now quite paranoid about making sure my interventions clearly indicate what the baseline measure is and what I expect the outcomes will be and how they will be both measured and 'judged' (or scaled).

I've seen, and used, a variety of methods for recording provisions and it is fair to say that one size never fits all. Whilst many software solutions have everything I NEED they do not have everything I WANT. I overcome this using any file attachment features. Other schools tell me that there is too much information on their provision maps and they scale it back to a list of pupils against the name of an intervention. I'm not sure how they do their financial accounting or make decisions about the success of provisions if that is the case, but that's not really for me to question.

I've included here some of the proformas for provision mapping that I've seen in use over time. I still tend to attach the 'Provision Information Document' as a file to my provisions – but like I say, I'm slightly paranoid! Blank versions are available at the back of the book.

Provision Information Document

Title	What is the name of the intervention? – Something everyone will recognise it by. Not ambiguous (e.g. "1:1") but not too specific (e.g 1:1 in-class toileting support for Fred)
Aims	What is this intervention for? What do we want to achieve? Why are we putting it in place? This can often be copied and pasted from the website of published resources.
What is this intervention?	What will happen? You don't need a set of lesson plans but an overview would be useful. Is it adult led or computer based?
Who is this aimed at?	Who will access this intervention? Is it a particular year group that can/will access it? Is it gender-specific?
What are the entry requirements (baseline)?	Do children need to be above a certain level to be able to access the intervention, or be below a certain level? How will you measure the baseline for the intervention?
What assessments are needed?	What assessment information will you use? Do you need to do a unique assessment? Who will do it? Where will the results be stored? How does the assessment result relate to the intervention?
What are the exit criteria?	Do you need to achieve a level before the intervention stops? Will you exit at the completion of the program? How is progress measured? What happens if progress isn't as expected does it continue, repeat or change?
Where will it take place?	What is the physical location of the intervention?

When?	When will the intervention take place? Start date...end date? Time of day?
How long will it take?	How many sessions and how long is each session?
Who will facilitate?	What staff are needed?
What resources are required?	What costs are involved? What 'free' items are involved? What did you buy last term that can be reused and therefore has no 'cost' attached? Where are physical resources stored?

FIXED	PUPIL	SESSION	OTHER
Staff training Group resources Reusable resources	Consumable resources Individual resources Photocopies	Staff costs Room costs	Any other related costs

OR

STAFF	RESOURCES	OTHER
Staff costs	Equipment Books, Consumable and Reusable resource costs	Any other related costs

How will it be monitored?	How will progress be monitored. How often, when, literally how? Will you look at data or do an observation? Is there any record keeping required?

Who will monitor?	Who will check up on the facilitator and pupils? Will it be the SENDCO, the class teacher, subject teacher, a combination?
Who do we need to inform?	Will the child be withdrawn from lessons? Who will this affect? How and when will you inform parents?
What information will class/subject teachers need?	What information are we going to feedback? Will they be involved? Can they apply the skills learned on an ongoing basis in their lessons? What transferable skills will pupils display at the end of the interventions? Are there any special techniques/methods staff should be aware of? Have you made parents aware, is there any follow-up homework they can do to support? Will they receive an 'intervention report'?

Session Intervention Records

Session Records for intervention:	Are they really necessary? What will you record if required? Who is the record for and when they get it will they have the time to read and act on it. Are they needed every session or perhaps once every 5 sessions for a daily intervention?
Why	Why are you recording information? Who is it for? What will it be used for? When will they have time to look at it? Will any action be taken on comments made? Who by? When?
Who	You might want to record any absences. This will impact on progress. Any change of staff for a session may need recording, this may account for any anomalies
What	Does each session have a specific focus (eg a phonic sound)? You could 'record' a session plan – objectives. This might be provided in a teacher resource guide. What happened in the session – planned or unplanned?
Where	Did the session take place in the normal location? Were there any interruptions?
When	Did the timing of the session cause any problems? Was the session cut short? Did pupils resent missing a particular session to attend? Is it always at the same time? Is this the best time?
How	How are you going to record the information? A post-it note, verbal feedback to the teacher/SENDCO, a record sheet, a note in a diary/planner, comments on a formal (or informal) session plan, electronic notes, an interim 'review', an email
Explain/Evaluate	Did anything unusual happen? Fire alarm? End evaluation

Manage it

Provision management is a strategic management approach which provides an 'at a glance' way of showing all the provision that the school makes which is additional to and different from that which is offered through the school's differentiated curriculum.

As I've already mentioned, having and putting into place the interventions is one thing (mapping) actually doing something with the information is another beast (management). This is suggested on p22-23.

Provision management starts with reviewing the information from the provision and then making decisions. I've already stated that it is important to look at the intervention as it is running and not wait until the end, but let's assume we've been doing that and we're now at the end of an intervention period looking at both the pupil plan (targets) and the provision (general financial value.)

Once the review is completed we need to report on the results to a variety of stake-holders and consider whether our interventions were 'value for money'.

Reviewing

Going back to the original information collected in the assess stage and looking for changes we are able to start a formal process of reviewing the success of the interventions and the progress of the pupils. This is the final named stage of the graduated approach and is often the one we have the least energy for. If we don't plan carefully, the assessment cycle can mean it falls at the end of term and we are busy chasing around for data and other bits of information whilst being generally shattered from the term itself! This is why, it is important to consider your SENDCO year and block the time in to do this around other events, but also to line up data collections so that much of the gathering is done at the same time.

Once you've collected the data you've not only got to read it and make some judgements but also report on it and make some decisions about next steps. If you refer back to page 13 the results of the intervention period can help us decide what happens within the graduated approach. We adjust the data and targets and start the cycle again, or (hopefully) celebrate success and cease the cycle.

Let's have a look at some examples:

PUPILS

Molly has been working towards her targets for 6 weeks (half a term). It is parents' evening and as SENDCO we have an appointment to review and renew her plan. (By the way, if you are doing this kind of thing at an open/parents' evening, it is important to have a sufficiently private space and adequate time along with all the required data to hand.). If you recall, Molly was new to our school and we had agreed to do some additional assessments in order to build a more detailed picture of her needs. We had set a quick plan in place for the meantime and we've been monitoring Molly. We will be discussing:

Feedback on targets and school interventions

Results of the agreed assessments

Suggested new interventions

Parental input and update

Pupil input and update

Agreed new targets and review date.

PROVISION

It's the end of term. We've collected all data and input it against our provisions. This is our Dockside intervention. Was it successful? For everyone? Would we change anything? At the end of this chapter I've included a review sheet for provisions with lots of questions you might like to ask yourself.

This is where I love my software package as I only collect data once and it feeds into both pupil plans and provisions meaning I don't have to flick between them hunting down results.

Evaluating Interventions

Evaluating Interventions	What do we do when we get to the end?
Who	Did we target the right pupils? How do you know? What is the evidence? Did we use the right staffing? How do you know? Where is the evidence? Was the right person doing the monitoring? Who made progress, who didn't? Are there any characteristics of the group? Did it work better for boys than girls?
When	Was this the right time for the intervention? Look at the time of year (impact of school events), the timing for individual pupils (do they need a settling period, were they ready for the intervention, should it be delivered to a younger group or earlier in their school career or do they need more maturity to access), was it the right time of day (impact on lessons missed, are they settled right after break, are they too hungry just before lunch)? How do you know it would be better/worse if moved to a different time? Was the monitoring at the right time? Was the reassessment at the right time? Assessment was completed at the end of the sessions, is it worth re-checking after a period of time? Are the skills retained?
Where	Was it the right location? How do you know? What about where the resources were located, was this appropriate? Would the intervention be more effective if delivered somewhere else?
What	Did we deliver what we set out to deliver? Was the program appropriate to meet the final objectives? What lessons have been learned about the intervention? What needs to change before the next delivery? What are the transferable skills? Pupil have made progress on an assessment but how do we know they are transferring skills to the curriculum and beyond?
How	Was the approach appropriate? Was adaptation needed? How do parents feel about the intervention? How do pupils feel about the intervention? How do staff feel about the intervention?
Why	Will you run this intervention again? Why?
Explain	Was this intervention cost effective?

Reporting

How you decide to report and who you report to will depend upon...you guessed it, your school! I remember cycle after cycle where everyone was so pressed with other priorities they just weren't interested in my information. I also recall returning from a short maternity leave (3-weeks!) and being asked for a report on my first day back because it suited someone else's agenda! These days, I generate the reports as a matter of course and file them for whoever needs them. (Actually, that's not strictly true, my software package does it for me with the click of a few buttons, I just have to add the dialogue when needed!)

What would we report on, how, why and to who/by whom?

Each audience will have its own requirements.

Parents/Pupils

In this situation you are looking back to however you undertook your assessment of the pupil and the targets you set out to achieve. You are reporting on their progress towards those targets and establishing what need to happen next. We would hope to report on successes, stating that the pupil has received 'this support' and their results now show 'this'. However, it can be just as valuable, and not at all negative, to have poor results or undesirable feedback about the success of an intervention. This is invaluable for families seeking support with a diagnosis and fighting against a system that says certain things need to be tried/happen before they can access services. Whilst our instinct is to want to give the positive information and show how great we are, in some cases (and they are rare) it is worth far more to the pupil to be able to state that intervention X did not work and therefore the school/pupil/family needs further advice and support from person/service Y. This can often work in your favour as a school when trying to access Element 3 (top-up/high level needs) funding, although do not make it a habit and certainly do not deliberately set a pupil up to 'fail' an intervention just for this purpose.

The language you use when speaking to parents will be different to that used with other professionals. Often the feedback will be verbal with perhaps a copy of the written notes showing any recently collected outcomes data.

Who provides this feedback? Ideally, the teachers involved in its delivery – so in our previous example it would have been the science teacher feeing back about their work towards the spelling targets, and both the English and Humanities departments contributing. In reality, it is probably the SENDCO who will collect the information and feedback during an additional meeting or telephone call. This is quite simply because secondary schools rarely meet parents more than once a year and we need to review the provision for pupils at least three times a year. In a primary school, where teachers usually see parents 2 or 3 times a year, it usually falls to the class teacher, possibly supported by the TA and maybe the SENDCO.

The result of this review and report will be comments from the pupil and parents which need to be recorded, along with your agreed next steps.

For me, with my 'plans' it simply meant adjusting any baseline data, setting new targets and agreeing what we would put in place next.

It is not usual to share financial information with parents around the cost of their child's interventions and it is certainly not appropriate to share the results or information of other pupils. So, if you are drawing together reports from a variety of sources you will need to consider how to do this without including information you perhaps do not want to share.

I consider myself a highly competent user of Access databases and Excel spreadsheets along with mail merge in Word, but I do prefer a commercial program to generate my reports for me as they simply gather all the input information and produce the report without any fussing! Not only that, by sharing access to the system other staff can enter the data saving me a lot of time collecting and collating it and they are pretty nifty at removing data about other pupils.

At the end of the school year, parents often receive a written school report about their child's progress in each subject (the quality of which can be eye-wateringly different!) and some schools opt to add out of class intervention reports to this formal document. Again, this can be really helpful to families of high needs pupils in that all their data Andi= information they need is in once place and a similar format.

School Staff (the delivery & teaching team)
We have managed to get our school staff engaged in the provision for our SEN pupils, so now we need to share the data. It can be really helpful for the maths department to see the results of the English intervention (for example) and draw information from it that might help with future support for an individual or for a group. Ideally, they shouldn't have to wait for a report to find out what has been happening, but it can serve as a useful review. It is important not to forget those staff who have been involved in the delivery (TAs), they also need feedback on whether the pupils and provisions have been successful. This group don't need an accurate financial breakdown, but you could use something similar to the Education Endowment Fund (EEF) to indicate high, medium and low cost in order to justify/explain decisions about removing or adding certain provisions.

School Staff (the SLT)
This group of individuals will want to know what is going on so they can prioritise school needs. They are going to be mainly interested in outcomes (as a general figure) and costs. They are the first of our groups who will use the phrase value for money. So, if you can justify the very expensive intervention that now means every pupil has an excellent reading age above average in just 3 months and they've sustained that outcome then 'go for it'! – it's cheaper than 5 years of intervention with limited impact, poor sustainability beyond the now and a lack of independent application from your pupils. (Can you message me the name of this excellent intervention?)

The SLT may also be interested in data from a performance management perspective. Not only will they want to check the reports against your work but individual teachers may have SEN related performance management objectives which can be quantified. Less often, although too frequent, they may be looking to cull staffing and sadly, TAs do tend to be in the firing line. Where hard evidence is required in making selecting staff to consider the data from 'who delivered value for money successful interventions' may be requested.

Governors
This diverse group will also be interested in value for money. Outcomes and finances are their focus and whilst they will hold the Head Teacher accountable it will all come back to you. Reports to governors need to be anonymised where possible (now you know why we don't call an intervention "1:1 support for Fred (Y1) toileting."). These reports tend to be the most narrative in explanation. Firstly, you are not likely to be at a meeting where they are discussed. Secondly, governors get reports before meetings and a table of data just generates too any questions. (Having been a governor for many years, please be advised they do not remember one report to the next what abbreviations stand for.)

OFSTED
As stated earlier this group will look at value for money, but actually it is outcomes they are most interested in. Case studies can be particularly helpful with this group accompanied by 'full reports'. Case studies can provide a useful narrative and, dare I say it, can help detract from not so positive data by providing a bigger picture. Unless you are under close scrutiny they don't have the time to read lots so a straightforward grid with colour coding would be helpful. However, if your data isn't looking too great, don't fill your page with 'red', find another way (numbers) or use more than 3 colours. (Did I really just tell you how to distract someone from the data?)

Other Professionals
You may need to produce reports for your local authority if you are requesting additional funding. Sometimes, if you apply to external funding or awarding bodies they will want to know what you put in place and why/if successful. Often these reports are generated for an individual pupil but I have been asked for a class comparative and also information about my year group and school.

For an individual pupil I am usually asked for details of interventions, frequency, duration, staff:pupil ratio and cost when submitting a funding bid. For an EHC Plan request it is likely I'd be asked all of the above plus a history of interventions (not normally with costs) and their outcomes.

Website

You have a duty to report on SEN progress on your school website. Whilst you do not have to report on SEN funding, you do need to report on PP expenditure and most schools will apply PP interventions alongside their SEN provision mapping. It is easy to upload an anonymised provision map (remember not to use pupil names for the titles of interventions) of all your interventions to the website so that parents are able to see the interventions that go above and beyond the quality classroom teaching that you offer. It may not be quite so helpful to include information about the spelling interventions offered by our English, Humanities and Science team in this report – but a more general statement about quality first teaching (wave 1) would cover this.

Yourself

Ultimately, you don't need a report as you have all the information and reports for everyone else...but you may need something for any accreditation you wish to apply for or for personal CPD and performance management.

If you recall, I prefer a commercial version of reporting and I include a few screen shots of the types of reports I can generate.

This first report shows the cost of interventions for my pupils. It might be something I use for SLT or when analysing for myself. If I needed a cost breakdown for my local authority I could remove pupil names or only generate the report for specific individuals. (I remember once being asked by SLT for a costs report for all Y8 PP, White British boys compared to non-white British...I really wouldn't fancy crunching that data from Excel.)

It is likely that I need to add an explanation narrative to any report I create. In this case it might be as straightforward as a sentence stating that the comprehension interventions is considerably more expensive than the SEAL focus group.

From 1/9/2017 to 1/9/2018

Breakdown by provision and pupil

	Pupils	Cost per pupil	Total
1:1 Dockside Comprehension			
Mandy Candy	1	172.02	172.02
Milly Candy	1	172.02	172.02
Molly Candy	1	172.02	172.02
Total	3	172.02	516.06
SEAL focus group - Managing Strong Feelings			
Mandy Candy	1	75.00	75.00
Milly Candy	1	75.00	75.00
Molly Candy	1	75.00	75.00
Total	3	75.00	225.00
Total	3	247.02	741.06

The second report looks at just one pupil and states their interventions, the costs associated, and where it has been reviewed the outcome (I use a scaling system from -2 to +2 based on Gauss analysis). I might use this with school staff, as a case study, or submit to the local authority as part of an Element 3 funding bid.

Although her second intervention has no outcome here, let's imagine it was scaled a -2. In combination with the previous report I can now state that the more expensive intervention was less successful that the other.

(A little silly since they're addressing different needs, but you get the gist, I'm sure.)

My third offering on the next page, could be a single pupil's diet of interventions over the course of the last academic year. It might be used to support an element 3 funding bid or an EHCP request. I am able to see what is being put in place, what the pupils:staff ratio is and how many hours they are receiving.

I used to sit on an Element 3 funding panel for my local authority and it never ceased to amaze me how many pupils would apparently receive 40 hours of intervention and be in their mainstream classes at the same time during a 25 hour teaching week! (This example illustrates that exact point since 954 hours of 1:1 in-class support accounts for just over 5 hours a day over 190 teaching days!)

Provision	Pupils	Pupil to staff ratio	Frequency	Total time allocated
Coping with Stress	8	1:1	1 per day	2 hours
Emotional Literacy	1	1:1	1 per day	20 hours
Memory Training	8	1:1	1 per day	7 hours
Numeracy 1:1 intervention	1	0.5:1	1 per day	49 hours
SLT Narrative Group	12	no staff	1 per week	20 hours
Precision Teaching	1	1:1	4 per week	39 hours
Positive Social Skills	6	1:1	1 per day	20 hours
In Class Support	1	1:1	1 per day	954 hours
Dictaphone Provision	1	no staff	-	-
Technology Provision	1	1:1	-	-
Behaviour Support Team Mentor	2	2:1	1 per day	9 hours
Plus 1	6	1:1	1 per day	-
Jigsaw Emotional Literacy	1	1:1	1 per week	10 hours

Conclusion

I'm hoping someone made it to the end of the book and the content has been helpful.

As I stated in the introduction, I'm not going to write and paint a wonderfully glowing picture of excellence, I can only point you in the direction of good practice whilst at the same time delivering a healthy dose of realism,

Appendix

Blank Provision Grid

Title	Description	Intended Outcome		
Area of Need	Wave	Start Date	End Date	Session length
Fixed costs	Per pupil costs	Per session Costs	Other costs	Session frequency
Total Cost	Cost per pupil	Other information		
Who will deliver	Ratio of support			
Who is in this intervention?	Group	Baseline data	Outcomes	Notes

Provision Information Document

Title	
Aims	
What is this intervention?	
Who is this aimed at?	
What are the entry requirements (baseline)?	
What assessments are needed?	
What are the exit criteria?	
Where will it take place?	

When?	
How long will it take?	
Who will facilitate?	
What resources are required?	

FIXED	PUPIL	SESSION	OTHER

OR

STAFF	RESOURCES	OTHER

How will it be monitored?	
Who will monitor?	

Who do we need to inform?	
What information will class/subject teachers need?	

Session Intervention Records

Session Records for intervention:	
Why	
Who	
What	
Where	
When	
How	
Explain/Evaluate	

Provision Mapping in Classrooms

Teacher		Group		Subject		Any additional support? Used for?	
Date From		Date To					

Who	Barriers	Targets	What I'll do	Resources	Baseline	Outcome

Provision Mapping on Medium-term Plans

Title		Year	Subject	Topic
Session	Objectives	Delivery		Modification
1				
2				
3				

Evaluating Interventions

Evaluating Interventions	
Who	
When	
Where	
What	
How	
Why	
Explain	

Books/Sites I suggest:

Natalie Packer: The Perfect SENCO

978-1781351048

Bob Bates: Quick Guide to Special Needs and Disabilities

978-1473979741

Anne Massey: Provision Mapping and the SEND Code of Practice

978-1138907089

SEND Code of Practice (0-25) 2015:

https://www.gov.uk/government/publications/send-code-of-practice-0-to-25

Edukey Education Limited

www.edukey.co.uk

(The specific program I used was Learning Plans and Provision Maps)

NASEN

Gold members of NASEN can access an excellent recording of their webinar: Provision Mapping and Management

About the Author

Abigail Hawkins is the Director at SENDCO Solutions. She works as the in-house SENDCO and DSL consultant with Edukey Education Ltd.

About SENDCO Solutions... Abigail Hawkins was a SENDCO for over 20 years of her teaching career. With experience across the whole age range (from 2 years to adults) and across a wide variety of settings and subjects, she is well placed to provide SEN advice for SENDCOs who have simply run out of ideas/juice! Whether you need a shoulder to cry on, a sympathetic ear, support with processes or paperwork, planning for the future, or fighting the current fire, Abigail can provide the advice and support you need to succeed in your role.

The SENDCO's SENDCO

www.sendcosolutions.co.uk

abigail@sendcosolutions.co.uk

.

Printed in Great Britain
by Amazon